W9-AUY-201

LLOYD D. NEWELL AND ROBERT L. MILLET

A Lamp Unto My Feet

DAILY REFLECTIONS ON THE OLD TESTAMENT

SALT LAKE CITY, UTAH

Visit us at deseretbook.com

Library of Congress Cataloging-in-Publication Data

Newell, Lloyd D., 1956–
A lamp unto my feet : daily reflections on the Old Testament / Lloyd D. Newell Robert L. Millet.
p. cm.
Includes bibliographical references.
ISBN 1-59038-483-0 (hardbound : alk. paper)
1 Bible. O.T.—Devotional literature. 2. Devotional calendars—Church of Jesus Christ of Latter-day Saints. 3. Church of Jesus Christ of Latter-day Saints—Prayer-books and devotions—English. I. Millet, Robert L. II. Title.
BS1151.55.N49 2005
242′.2—dc22 2005017655

Printed in the United States of America 42316
Inland Press, Menomonee Falls, WI

10 9 8 7 6 5 4 3 2 1

The Psalmist mirrored the deep feelings of our heart as authors when he wrote of the blessing of posterity: "Lo, children are an heritage of the Lord: and the fruit of the womb is his reward. . . . Happy is the man that hath his quiver full of them" (Psalm 127:3, 5). This book is dedicated affectionately to our children, who have brought us a great deal of satisfaction and joy.

THE NEWELLS	THE MILLETS
Hayley	*Angie*
McKay	*David*
Abby	*Michael*
Jacob	*Jeff*
	Becky
	Stephen

Preface

As a brief guided tour of the Old Testament, from Genesis through Malachi, *A Lamp Unto My Feet* is an invitation to reflect seriously on the sweet and sobering word of God. "The law of the Lord is perfect," the Psalmist wrote, "converting the soul: the testimony of the Lord is sure, making wise the simple. The statutes of the Lord are right, rejoicing the heart: the commandment of the Lord is pure, enlightening the eyes. The fear of the Lord is clean, enduring for ever: the judgments of the Lord are true and righteous altogether. More to be desired are they than gold, yea, than much fine gold: sweeter also than honey and the honeycomb" (Psalm 19:7–10).

In the preparation of this volume, we are indebted to many people. Jana Erickson offered enthusiastic encouragement from the beginning. Christine Ipson tenaciously tracked down references and organized files. Lori Soza succeeded at the daunting task of compiling and ordering the separate days into a cohesive whole. Suzanne Brady has, as always, provided her substantive but sensitive editorial touch, which simply has made this a better book. We are particularly grateful for our wives, Karmel and Shauna, and for their ongoing support through a demanding time. The peaceful environments in our homes make the difficult task of writing much, much more manageable.

JANUARY

So God created man in his own image,
in the image of God created he him; male
and female created he them.

GENESIS 1:27

JANUARY 1

In the beginning God created the heaven and the earth.

GENESIS 1:1

Fundamental to a serious understanding of the place of mankind on earth, and of our possibilities here and hereafter, is the idea that we were created by God. Mankind was not made from nothing, nor are we a product of chance occurrences. Joseph Smith the Prophet taught: "Everlasting covenant was made between three personages before the organization of this earth, and relates to their dispensation of things to men on the earth; these personages, according to Abraham's record, are called God the first, the Creator; God the second, the Redeemer; and God the third, the witness or Testator" (*Teachings,* 190). Our Heavenly Father created us, and thus our connection to the heavens and the heavenly is more direct than many have ever supposed.

JANUARY 2

So God created man in his own image,
in the image of God created he him; male and
female created he them.
GENESIS 1:27

The Proclamation on the Family states: "All human beings—male and female—are created in the image of God. Each is a beloved spirit son or daughter of heavenly parents, and, as such, each has a divine nature and destiny" (*Ensign,* November 1995, 102). No more supernal truth has ever been uttered by the prophets of God. Eliza R. Snow wrote poetically in "O My Father":

In the heav'ns are parents single?
No, the thought makes reason stare!
Truth is reason; truth eternal
Tells me I've a mother there. (Hymns, *no. 292*)

This truth, so simple, yet so very profound, changes how we see ourselves and others and how we view God and his great plan of happiness for us, his children. When we truly comprehend who we are and from whence we came, we understand that we have something of divinity within us—a divine nature and destiny. We are God's great and final creation, his beloved sons and daughters.

JANUARY 3

Be fruitful, and multiply, and replenish the earth, and subdue it: and have dominion over the fish of the sea, and over the fowl of the air, and over every living thing that moveth upon the earth.

GENESIS 1:28

The commandment to Adam and Eve and their descendants to be like their heavenly parents in the procreative process is the most sacred stewardship of life. Prophets have said in our day, "We declare that God's commandment for His children to multiply and replenish the earth remains in force. We further declare that God has commanded that the sacred powers of procreation are to be employed only between man and woman, lawfully wedded as husband and wife" ("The Family: A Proclamation," *Ensign,* November 1995, 102). Long ago, Nephi wrote, "The Lord hath created the earth that it should be inhabited; and he hath created his children that they should possess it" (1 Nephi 17:36). The blessing and privilege to create bodies for God's spirit children is a sacred responsibility. Likewise, it is a solemn duty to be wise stewards of the earth, to live in righteous rulership over the earth. As we do so, we become more like our Father in Heaven.

JANUARY 4

And God saw every thing that he had made, and, behold, it was very good.

GENESIS 1:31

Everything that comes from God is good. He who is perfect in all things and perfectly good in all ways cannot produce that which is bad. The Pearl of Great Price gives us an account of God's appraisal of Creation: "I, God, saw everything that I had made, and, behold, all things which I had made were very good" (Moses 2:31). God has created the heaven and the earth, the sun and moon and stars, and all living things—and they are very good. He has created his beloved children, each one with a divine nature and destiny—and they are very good. All things that come from God are good. We are his sons and daughters, endowed with the seeds of godhood. We are to be partakers of the divine nature (2 Peter 1:4), to become more like our Father in Heaven, to strive to put off the natural man and become fully good and perfect, even as he is (Matthew 5:48; Mosiah 3:19).

JANUARY 5

And God blessed the seventh day, and sanctified it: because that in it he had rested from all his work which God created and made.

GENESIS 2:3

The weekly Sabbath is set apart so that we, like God at the creation of the earth, might rest from our labors for a day. It was instituted to commemorate God's seventh day of rest at the Creation (Exodus 20:10–11), the deliverance of Israel from Egyptian bondage (Deuteronomy 5:15), and Christ's resurrection from the dead. It is a holy day set apart for us to more fully contemplate the things of eternity, to gather with other Saints to worship, to reach out in love and service to others, and to grow spiritually as we strive to keep ourselves unspotted from the world (D&C 59:9–15). It is a day of rest, rejuvenation, and recommitment to the principles of the gospel. Keeping the Sabbath day holy is important enough to God that it is one of the Ten Commandments. It ought to be important enough to us that we honor this holy day with our actions and attitudes.

JANUARY 6

And the Lord God formed man of the dust of the ground, and breathed into his nostrils the breath of life; and man became a living soul.

GENESIS 2:7

Speaking of the creation of Adam and Eve, President Spencer W. Kimball said: "Man became a living soul—mankind, male and female. The Creators breathed into their nostrils the breath of life and man and woman became living souls. We don't know exactly how their coming into this world happened, and when we're able to understand it the Lord will tell us" (*Ensign,* March 1976, 72). Although we do not know all the particulars about our first ancestors, we do know that they were sealed for eternity in the Garden of Eden; they are not mere legend and folklore; they actually walked this earth and lived and taught the gospel of Jesus Christ; they are the father and mother, the patriarch and matriarch, of the human race on the earth; and together they will share eternal glory. As their descendants we honor their names, for they are foremost among the noble and great.

JANUARY 7

And the Lord God said, It is not good that the man should be alone; I will make him an help meet for him.
GENESIS 2:18

In the divine plan men and women have differing natures and roles, but nothing in scripture or prophetic statement suggests that either male or female is superior to the other; rather, they are complementary. Eve was not an afterthought nor just a good idea conceived by God when he wondered what else might be added to his grand creation. Adam and Eve were a package, a team, a partnership from the beginning. Eve was a help meet suited to, worthy of, and equal to the task of putting the great plan of happiness into effect and making mortality possible. Thus, in the words of the apostle Paul, "neither is the man without the woman, neither the woman without the man, in the Lord" (1 Corinthians 11:11). Neither male nor female can enjoy without the other the ultimate blessings of eternal life in the world to come.

JANUARY 8

Therefore shall a man leave his father and his mother, and shall cleave unto his wife: and they shall be one flesh.

GENESIS 2:24

Truth concerning the everlasting covenant of marriage comes from the Lord. His message of oneness in marriage has always been the same (Matthew 19:5–6). He says that to enter into the everlasting covenant of marriage, the husband and wife must leave their parents and cleave to each other. To cleave to one's spouse means to adhere to each other unwaveringly, to be faithful in thought and deed, to honor marital covenants with complete fidelity. It means husband and wife should each occupy first place in the affections, interests, and loyalties of the other—before parents, children, friends, callings, and other associations and responsibilities. To be one in marriage and enjoy its fulness signifies that each spouse selflessly puts the other first and cherishes the joy and blessing of growing together in the marital covenant. Only the Lord comes before our spouse. And if we truly put the Lord first in our lives, we will regard and treat our spouse as preeminent in our lives.

JANUARY 9

And he said unto the woman, Yea, hath God said, Ye shall not eat of every tree of the garden?

GENESIS 3:1

The fall of our first parents was as much a part of the divine plan as was the Atonement. In truth, Adam and Eve went into the Garden to fall. "Adam fell that men might be," Lehi observed, "and men are, that they might have joy" (2 Nephi 2:25). The actions of Adam and Eve in Eden were a transgression, not a sin, for "Adam was made to open the way of the world" (Smith, *Teachings,* 12). Elder Orson F. Whitney taught: "The fall had a twofold direction—downward, yet forward. It brought man into the world and set his feet upon progression's highway" (*Cowley and Whitney on Doctrine,* 287). In essence, God said to Adam and Eve, "If you want to stay in the Garden of Eden, then do not eat the fruit. If you choose to take the fruit, you cannot remain in the garden." The Atonement was the child of the Fall, and the Atonement opens us to endless and eternal possibilities.

JANUARY 10

And the Lord God called unto Adam,
and said unto him, Where art thou?
GENESIS 3:9

Philosophers and theologians for centuries have debated this fascinating question: "Adam, . . . Where art thou?" How, they ask, could an all-wise, all-knowing Deity pose such a question? Did the Father of heaven and earth not know where Adam and Eve were, or is the query merely rhetorical? Yet there is profound meaning in the question. In the first place, God was calling for an accounting from our first parents—an explanation for what they had done and where they now stood before him. In like fashion, God calls to each one of us by name: Where are you, Bill? Where are you going, Elizabeth? In short, where are we in regard to where we ought to be? The answer is essential to our progress in returning Home.

JANUARY 11

And I will put enmity between thee and the woman, and between thy seed and her seed; it shall bruise thy head, and thou shalt bruise his heel.

GENESIS 3:15

Lucifer, the father of all lies, is the sworn enemy of God and the plan of salvation. Because of Satan's darkened condition, he desires to thwart that plan and thus bring misery upon all of God's children, the same misery he will enjoy everlastingly. Satan has, from the foundation of the world, demonstrated animosity toward the Father and the Son. And yet, though the devil will bruise the heel of the Savior—"the seed of the woman"—in the end, our Lord will crush the serpent's head, that is, he shall defeat the forces of evil and create heaven on earth. "Salvation is nothing more nor less," the Prophet Joseph explained, "than to triumph over all our enemies and put them under our feet. And when we have power to put all enemies under our feet in this world, and a knowledge to triumph over all evil spirits in the world to come, then we are saved" (*Teachings,* 297).

JANUARY 12

In sorrow thou shalt bring forth children; and thy desire shall be to thy husband, and he shall rule over thee.

GENESIS 3:16

President Spencer W. Kimball declared: "The Lord said to the woman: ' . . . in sorrow thou shalt bring forth children.' . . . The term *distress* instead of sorrow . . . would mean much the same, except I think there is great gladness in most Latter-day Saint homes when there is to be a child there. As he concludes this statement he says, 'and thy desire shall be to thy husband, and he shall rule over thee.' (Gen. 3:16.) I have a question about the word *rule.* It gives the wrong impression. I would prefer to use the word *preside* because that's what he does. A righteous husband presides over his wife and family" (*Ensign,* March 1976, 72). Father and mother, husband and wife, are equal partners with sacred responsibilities: hers, to give birth and nurture; his, to preside, provide, and protect in love and righteousness ("The Family: A Proclamation," *Ensign,* November 1995, 102). Side by side they walk together into eternity.

JANUARY 13

Unto Adam also and to his wife did the Lord God make coats of skins, and clothed them.

GENESIS 3:21

Once Adam and Eve became mortal, the Lord did not leave them to figure out how to cover their sacred bodies. Fig leaves were not good enough for his most glorious creations. Tenderly, he taught Adam and Eve about the temporal matter of dressing modestly. The Lord who "looketh on the heart" (1 Samuel 16:7) understands the importance of covering our bodies so others are more apt to look upon our hearts than to be distracted by our bodies. When we dress modestly, we help those around us to have pure thoughts. We also show respect to ourselves and to the God who made us. In later dispensations, he would warn his children not to be "lifted up in the pride of your hearts . . . because of the costliness of your apparel" (Jacob 2:13). He would also caution against excess: "Let all thy garments be plain, and their beauty the beauty of the work of thine own hands" (D&C 42:40).

JANUARY 14

Therefore the Lord God sent him forth from the garden of Eden, to till the ground from whence he was taken.

GENESIS 3:23

Adam and Eve were driven out of the garden to a telestial land of thorns and thistles, where they would eat bread by the sweat of their brow (Genesis 3:18–19). But the Lord knew that his punishment of Adam and Eve would lead to their spiritual growth and ultimate joy. It is in worthwhile work that we nurture the seeds of godliness within us. Physical labor and purposeful effort are spiritual necessities for those who would realize their true potential and achieve everlasting happiness. The slothful and lazy are specifically condemned throughout scripture (Matthew 25:26; Alma 60:14; D&C 56:17; 107:100). It is not genius or good intentions that spell the difference in the man or woman of Christ. It is work. It is the willingness to be anxiously engaged, to put our shoulder to the wheel, to do our part to build both the kingdom and our character.

JANUARY 15

And the Lord said unto Cain, Where is Abel thy brother? And he said, I know not: Am I my brother's keeper?

GENESIS 4:9

Self-deception is the greatest of all lies. Cain lied to the Lord, to his family, and to himself. He thought he could literally get away with murder. But the Lord, who knows all things and all hearts, knew the truth. Liars may fool some of the people, even many people, for a season. Eventually, however, lies escalate, truth is exposed, and liars are caught in a fraudulent web of their own making. Pride, often manifest as greed and jealousy, is at the root of all lies. Like Cain, liars want to have more than their brother and better than their neighbor. They want to appear true when they are false, strong when they are weak, valiant when they are cowardly. They close their hearts to the whisperings of the Lord and the influence of righteous people, as they listen to the father of lies (Moses 5:26–30). The Saints of God are to be people of honesty and integrity, people who live truthfully.

JANUARY 16

And Enoch walked with God after he begat Methuselah three hundred years, and begat sons and daughters. . . . And Enoch walked with God: and he was not; for God took him.

GENESIS 5:22–24

Enoch is one of the enigmatic figures in antiquity. Legends and apocryphal stories have grown up about him for millennia. And yet few people know who he truly was, what he accomplished, and why he and his city stand as a scriptural prototype for all who seek after holiness. The book of Moses tells us that Enoch was called of God as a prophet; that he worked diligently with a sinful generation for some 365 years; and that because of the power of his presentation and the work of the priesthood in the earth, Zion was established, a city that was "of one heart and one mind, and dwelt in righteousness; and there was no poor among them" (Moses 7:18). Because of their unity and righteousness, they were taken from the earth, translated, without tasting death (Hebrews 11:5). All the prophets thereafter sought to follow the pattern of ancient Zion: They "looked for a city which hath foundations, whose builder and maker is God" (Hebrews 11:10).

JANUARY 17

And God saw that the wickedness of man was great in the earth, and that every imagination of the thoughts of his heart was only evil continually.

GENESIS 6:5

One can hardly imagine the mists of darkness that must have enshrouded the earth during the days of Noah, a time when, as Moses recorded, the people's hearts and imaginations were riveted to wickedness. One can understand why, in the divine providences of heaven, the Almighty chose to destroy the earth by water as a great act of mercy and love (Taylor, *Journal of Discourses,* 21:17–18; 22:301–2; 24:290–91). The Flood, in washing away the wicked, represents the baptism of the earth; symbolically, our sins are likewise washed away when we enter the waters of baptism (Acts 22:16; D&C 39:10). In a time not far distant, the Son of Man will come in power and great glory to cleanse the earth of evil once again, this time through the baptism of fire.

And I will make of thee a great nation, and I will bless thee, and make thy name great; and thou shalt be a blessing: and I will bless them that bless thee, and curse him that curseth thee: and in thee shall all families of the earth be blessed.

GENESIS 12:2–3

What we call the Abrahamic covenant is set forth in the book of Genesis (for example, Genesis 12; 15; 17). It is the gospel covenant, the new and everlasting covenant, the fulness of all God's covenants and ordinances. We call it the Abrahamic covenant in part because Abraham was a righteous soul who kept the gospel covenant faithfully. In addition, more is recorded about the covenant in God's dealings with Abraham than with any other prophet. God's "promises made to the fathers" (D&C 2:2) entail the following: Abraham's posterity is entitled to the gospel of Jesus Christ; his descendants will administer that gospel through the holy priesthood; the descendants of Abraham, Isaac, and Jacob are entitled to the blessings of eternal life, which includes a promise of an endless posterity and the continuation of the family unit in eternity; finally, the descendants of the father of the faithful are entitled to a land of promise (Abraham 2:8–11, 19).

JANUARY 19

And he believed in the Lord; and he counted it to him for righteousness.
GENESIS 15:6

To believe in the Lord, to believe in his promises and to trust in his tender mercies, is to have faith in him. Abraham knew by vision and revelation of the coming of the Lord Jesus Christ as the Messiah, the Lamb slain from the foundation of the world. God honored Abraham's belief and the faithfulness that followed such belief. Abraham's was a believing heart. He knew the Lord, and he knew the voice of the Lord. Thus when the command came to do the unspeakable, Abraham surely must have anguished over what he was called upon to do, but because he believed in the Lord, he went about the terrible task to which he had been called. Although, finally, it was not required of him to thrust the knife into his covenant son, the father of the faithful proceeded on that course until the angel of the Lord blocked the action and accepted Abraham's sacrifice in righteousness.

JANUARY 20

And when Abram was ninety years old and nine, the Lord appeared to Abram, and said unto him, I am the Almighty God; walk before me, and be thou perfect.

GENESIS 17:1

Our Heavenly Father can ask nothing but perfection from his children. That is the divine standard. On the one hand, we are to do all within our power to keep the commandments of God, to deny ourselves of all ungodliness and worldly lusts, and to give no heed to the taunts and invitations from the large and spacious building. But no one, not even the mightiest prophet or the greatest apostle, has lived a perfect life. Jesus alone was able to travel life's paths without a detour or a backward step spiritually. As we join Christ in covenant, we become perfect in him. We, the incomplete, join with him who is complete. We, the unfinished, join with him who is the finisher of our faith. We, the imperfect, join with him who is perfect, and we (Christ and you and I) become perfect. The celestial kingdom will be inhabited by those who have been "made perfect" through the application of his perfect atonement (D&C 76:69).

JANUARY 21

For I know him, that he will command his children and his household after him, and they shall keep the way of the Lord.

GENESIS 18:19

Abraham kept the commandments of God. He was faithful and trustworthy and dependable always, even on occasions when only God and Abraham knew what he did. Truly, his private victories prepared him for his public success. God spoke similarly to Nephi, son of Helaman: "Behold, I will bless thee forever; and I will make thee mighty in word and in deed, in faith and in works; yea, even that all things shall be done unto thee according to thy word, for thou shalt not ask that which is contrary to my will" (Helaman 10:5). God knew Abraham, and he knew Abraham's heart. He knew he could trust his servant implicitly to attend to sacred things, particularly those things that lead to exaltation and eternal life: the teaching and training of his children.

JANUARY 22

And it came to pass, when they had brought them forth abroad, that he said, Escape for thy life; look not behind thee, neither stay thou in all the plain; escape to the mountain, lest thou be consumed.

GENESIS 19:17

Jesus spoke often in the four Gospels of the cost of discipleship and of what it takes to be one of his serious and sincere followers (Luke 9:23). The story of Lot's family escaping the cities of the plain before their destruction is an actual account in human history. It is also symbolically representative of what each of us is called upon to do as we come out of the world of darkness into the marvelous light of Christ (1 Peter 2:9). We do not look back or fantasize about what life might have been like had we stayed; rather, we press on and leave Babylon behind. Too often, however, those who, like Lot's wife, are "a little tinctured with gentilism" drag their feet and delay the inevitable decision (Taylor, *Journal of Discourses,* 26:36). The ever-present command of the Almighty in both ancient and modern scripture is "Go ye out from Babylon; be ye clean that bear the vessels of the Lord" (D&C 133:5).

JANUARY 23

And Isaac brought her into his mother Sarah's tent, and took Rebekah, and she became his wife; and he loved her.

GENESIS 24:67

Isaac loved Rebekah. He was not simply possessed of a mystical force, emotional feeling, or biological drive. He made a covenant with her—the new and everlasting covenant of marriage—and his commitment to serve and honor her was one that he would keep all the days of his life. We can be certain that although Isaac was the ultimate presiding officer in his family, he and Rebekah were full partners in raising the family and conducting the business associated with daily living. Later, in Genesis 27, we learn of an instance in which Rebekah seems to have been more in tune with the Spirit than Isaac when it came to bestowing the birthright upon Jacob. This story in no way diminishes the greatness of Isaac but rather demonstrates a working spiritual partnership between a man and his wife who have now ascended to godhood (D&C 132:37).

JANUARY 24

Jacob said, Sell me this day thy birthright. And Esau said, Behold, I am at the point to die: and what profit shall this birthright do to me? . . . Then Jacob gave Esau bread and pottage of lentiles; and he did eat and drink, and rose up, and went his way.

GENESIS 25:31–34

The birthright entailed a double portion of property from the father and the right to hold the keys of the priesthood and be the overseer of that divine authority. In our Heavenly Father's family, Jehovah, who is Jesus Christ, is the oldest spirit child of the Father and is thus the one entitled to the birthright. Through the blessings of the gospel, including the receipt of temple covenants and ordinances, we open ourselves to inherit and receive equally with the Beloved Son. That is, through keeping our covenants we qualify to become joint heirs, or coinheritors, with Christ to all that the Father has. Jesus is the Firstborn, but by adoption and regeneration we may come to inherit thrones, kingdoms, principalities, and powers, just as he has. Those who so inherit will be known as the Church of the Firstborn.

JANUARY 25

And Rebekah spake unto Jacob her son, saying, Behold, I heard thy father speak unto Esau thy brother. . . . Now therefore, my son, obey my voice according to that which I command thee.

GENESIS 27:6–8

Isaac wanted the birthright to go to his favorite son, Esau, but Rebekah knew by revelation (Genesis 25:23) that the elder should serve the younger. Thus Jacob should bear the birthright. This is clearly a case in which Jacob was foreordained to stand as a great prophet-leader and become the head of the house of Israel. God will bring to pass his purposes in the earth—and that certainly includes getting the right people into the right place at the right time. The foreordination of Jacob (Israel) had been decreed from the foundations of the world, but for whatever reason, the otherwise righteous Isaac almost allowed his personal preference to preclude the plan of God. Thus what Rebekah did was neither deceitful nor sinful but a courageous and inspired action. She acted as she was moved upon by the Spirit of God (Erastus Snow, *Journal of Discourses,* 21:369–71).

JANUARY 26

And Rebekah said to Isaac, I am weary of my life because of the daughters of Heth: if Jacob take a wife of the daughters of Heth, such as these which are of the daughters of the land, what good shall my life do me?

GENESIS 27:46

Salvation is a family affair. If the greatest joys in life are family joys (and they are), then surely nothing is more painful than family pain. Much of what the ancients wrote in regard to the importance of having children and rearing a righteous posterity has been lost to our secular and distracted world. In our day many have lost track of what matters most, particularly in regard to marriage and family. The ancient Saints grasped the sober reality that to marry outside the gospel covenant was to transform what was intended to be a divine ordinance into a civil ceremony, one that ended at death. That is why Elder Bruce R. McConkie taught again and again that the single most important thing any Latter-day Saint ever does is to marry the right person in the right place by the right authority (*Choose an Eternal Companion,* n.p.). People matter, relationships are vital, and the family is intended to be forever.

JANUARY 27

And she conceived, and bare a son; and said, God hath taken away my reproach: and she called his name Joseph; and said, The Lord shall add to me another son.

GENESIS 30:23–24

As the scripture indicates, one meaning of the name *Joseph* is "to add or to add to." Jacob's beloved wife Rachel, who had had such difficulty bearing children, was blessed with a son, a special son, one destined to change the course of history. Some scholars believe that the word *Joseph* comes from a word that means "to gather." We learn later in the book of Genesis of Joseph's success in gathering his own family together. We learn more especially from the prophecies of Joseph about a latter-day seer by the name of Joseph who would be directly involved in the final great work of the gathering of Israel. Joseph Smith, the Choice Seer, was called to restore the fulness of the gospel, to gather the elect from the four corners of the earth (D&C 29:7), and thereby to prepare the Saints to stand upon Mount Zion in the great city of the New Jerusalem (D&C 84:2).

JANUARY 28

And Jacob was left alone; and there wrestled a man with him until the breaking of the day.

GENESIS 32:24

Each of us faces significant moments in life when challenges or questions drive us to our knees with an intensity that will not allow us to arise until an answer or a perspective has come. Enos wrestled with the Lord all day and into the night to obtain a remission of his sins (Enos 1:4). Of our Master's suffering in Gethsemane, Luke records, "And being in an agony he prayed more earnestly: and his sweat was as it were great drops of blood falling down to the ground" (Luke 22:44). Imagine! The Son of God, he who did all things right, prayed "more earnestly." Some tasks and challenges call forth the kind of prayer that draws upon the depths of the soul in order to make the proper connection with the Infinite.

JANUARY 29

And he dreamed yet another dream, and told it his brethren. . . . And he told it to his father. . . . And his brethren envied him; but his father observed the saying.

GENESIS 37:9–11

Joseph came to the earth with a gift for spirituality—the spiritual gift to receive prophetic dreams and through them to learn the mind and will of the Lord during the time he was asleep. As an inexperienced and perhaps somewhat naïve youngster in regard to spiritual gifts, he no doubt was eager to share with others what God had in store for his particular family. But his brothers, themselves lacking in many of their younger sibling's spiritual graces, resented Joseph's spirituality. So it was with Nephi, with Joseph Smith, and with others who fearlessly proclaim the word of God to an unprepared audience. There is a loneliness associated with spiritual leadership, a lonely path that the prophets of God in particular are called upon to walk. Learning eventually that they cannot share everything they receive, they learn discipline and discrimination as they are required to walk with God and live with man.

JANUARY 30

How then can I do this great wickedness, and sin against God?

GENESIS 39:9

The story of Joseph's resisting the enticements of Potiphar's wife is a timeless example of faith and personal purity. President Gordon B. Hinckley said: "Challenging though it may be, there is a way to apply traditional moral principles in our day. For some unknown reason, there is constantly appearing the false rationalization that at one time in the long-ago, virtue was easy and that now it is difficult. I would like to remind any who feel that way that there has never been a time since the Creation when the same forces were not at work that are at work today. The proposal made by Potiphar's wife to Joseph in Egypt is no different from that faced by many men and women and youth in our day" (*Ensign,* August 1988, 4). Our temptations may not be as dramatic as Joseph's, but they are real. Daily we must resist the carnal pull of the world and align ourselves with the Lord and the everlasting truth of his gospel.

JANUARY 31

And she caught him by his garment, saying, Lie with me: and he left his garment in her hand, and fled, and got him out.

GENESIS 39:12

The moment when Potiphar's wife caught hold of Joseph and urged him to sin with her was not a time for a reasoned conversation. This was not an occasion where the pure Joseph could sit down with Potiphar's wife, teach her the plan of salvation, explain the importance of virtue and chastity, and hope to witness a change in her heart and her passions. Joseph did what any self-respecting and self-disciplined, righteous person should do—he got out. We are called to flee fornication. Anyone who spends too much time lounging near the fascinating flame of sin will eventually be burned. Our call as disciples of the Holy One of Israel is to stay as far away from sin and its fellow travelers as we possibly can. None of us is immune to temptation, and none of us can "handle it" on our own. We would do well to avoid sin and even the very appearance of it (1 Thessalonians 5:22).

FEBRUARY

And ye shall be unto me a
kingdom of priests, and an holy nation.
EXODUS 19:6

FEBRUARY 1

And Pharaoh said unto his servants, Can we find such a one as this is, a man in whom the Spirit of God is?
GENESIS 41:38

Even those who are without the light of the fulness of the gospel can recognize the hand of God upon someone if they are open to such manifestations. Joseph's unusual gifts were recognized and used by Pharoah because Joseph chose to stand tall and to rise above the beggarly elements of this world. In him the Spirit of God dwelt. From him the Spirit of God emanated. Standing on higher ground, Joseph was able to lift other souls; having the fire of faith burning within his own heart, he was able to light that flame within others. Walking by the light of the Spirit of the Lord, he was able to save himself, his family, and an entire nation. Who can judge the infinite influence of a righteous and God-fearing man or woman?

The sceptre shall not depart from Judah, nor a lawgiver from between his feet, until Shiloh come; and unto him shall the gathering of the people be.

GENESIS 49:10

Jacob (Israel) pronounced on the head of his son Judah the right to a political kingdom. As promised in 2 Samuel 7, the person who presided as king in Jerusalem would be of the tribe of Judah. Jesus Christ was born of the tribe of Judah, and had the people lived in greater light and understanding, they would have recognized Jesus as their rightful king. In the future day when our Lord and Master governs the earth from two sites—from the New Jerusalem in Missouri, as well as from Old Jerusalem in the Holy Land—the prophecy of Isaiah will be fulfilled that "out of Zion shall go forth the law, and the word of the Lord from Jerusalem" (Isaiah 2:3). The true gathering of Israel was, is, and will forevermore be first and foremost to the Person of Jesus Christ and then, secondarily, to the lands of their inheritance.

FEBRUARY 3

Joseph is a fruitful bough, even a fruitful bough by a well; whose branches run over the wall. . . . The blessings of thy father . . . shall be on the head of Joseph, and on the crown of the head of him that was separate from his brethren.

GENESIS 49:22–26

The prophetic blessing of Joseph by his father, Jacob, (Israel) clearly alludes to a righteous branch of Joseph's posterity crossing the wall of water that separates the hemispheres and settling in a land that is choice above all other lands. The Nephite prophets and even the Savior himself reminded the descendants of Lehi that they were a prophetic people, who, as descendants of Joseph, were entitled to unspeakable blessings. That the blessings of Abraham, Isaac, and Jacob should spread "unto the utmost bound of the everlasting hills" (Genesis 29:26) refers to the movement of the Latter-day Saints across the plains of North America to the Great Basin, where they established Salt Lake City as the headquarters of the kingdom of God on earth. The ancient prophecies are being fulfilled as the Church and its influence continue to spread to every corner of the globe.

Now when Pharaoh heard this thing, he sought to slay Moses. But Moses fled from the face of Pharaoh, and dwelt in the land of Midian. Now Moses kept the flock of Jethro his father in law, the priest of Midian.

EXODUS 2:15; 3:1

Midian was a son of Abraham by his wife Keturah (Genesis 25:1–2). When Moses fled the court of Pharaoh, he "dwelt in the land of Midian" (Exodus 2:15), where he was ordained to the higher priesthood by Jethro, his father-in-law and "the priest of Midian" (Exodus 3:1; D&C 84:6). Doctrine and Covenants 107 records a priesthood lineage from Noah, Methuselah, Enoch, Jared, Seth, and Adam (D&C 107:41–52). This lineage is the birthright lineage through which these high priests served as presiding patriarchs and held the keys or right of presidency in their own dispensations. In another revelation on priesthood, Doctrine and Covenants 84, we note that Jethro's priesthood line came through Caleb, Elihu, Jeremy, Esaias, Abraham, Melchizedek, Noah, Enoch, Abel, and Adam. This suggests that there was more than one line of priesthood among the ancients, a simple principle but one unknown to those without the benefit of modern revelation.

FEBRUARY 5

And he said, Draw not nigh hither: put off thy shoes from off thy feet, for the place whereon thou standest is holy ground.

EXODUS 3:5

The God of Abraham, Isaac, and Jacob taught his prophet Moses a monumental lesson: One does not rush into the presence of the Almighty, nor does he take lightly the truth that communication with Deity is sacred and holy. Moses stood on holy ground because God was there. We likewise stand in holy places when we enter temples of the Lord, worship in dedicated chapels throughout the world, and strive to make our homes a bit of heaven on earth. We stand in holy places as we walk in the footsteps of our Master in the Holy Land, as we travel to where the early Latter-day Saints gave their lives and their all to lay the foundation for this latter-day work. And we stand in holy places to the extent that we live lives of holiness—deny ourselves of things alien to the Spirit of God, discern and eschew wicked practices in our day, and cleave tenaciously unto things of righteousness.

FEBRUARY 6

And Moses said unto God, Behold, when I come unto the children of Israel, and shall say unto them, The God of your fathers hath sent me unto you; and they shall say to me, What is his name? what shall I say unto them?

EXODUS 3:13

This passage gives rise to a whole host of questions. For example, did the elders of Israel know the name of the God they worshipped, and would they be testing Moses to see if he had actually been in the presence of that holy being? Or, did they not know the name of the Almighty—having perhaps lost that name through periods of apostasy—and were they thus anxious to relearn the holy name? Once again we are uncertain. One thing is clear from this passage, however, and that is the power to be had in a name, especially the name of God. Anciently it was believed that to know the name of an important person was to have power over or influence with that person. Thus to know the name of Deity was to better understand who he was, what his powers were, and how one might access those powers. In any fashion, Moses understood that his word would be tested by the elders of Israel and that he must be prepared to give the name of the God he represented.

And God said unto Moses, I AM THAT I AM:
and he said, Thus shalt thou say unto the children of Israel,
I AM hath sent me unto you.

EXODUS 3:14

The language of Exodus 3:14 speaks volumes about the nature of God and his attributes. In Hebrew the Lord's answer to Moses is *ehyeh asher ehyeh,* a play on the verb *to be* and related closely to the word *Yahweh,* the personal name of the God of the ancients. Commentators have for centuries discussed this passage and suggested various translations and explanations. Some say God is stating that he will be who he will be. Others say he is saying, "I am he who causes to be, he who brings into existence." Still others say he is saying, "I am the One who is, the self-existent one." Somehow the tradition had grown up among the Israelites—perhaps as an exaggeration of the command not to speak the name of the Lord in vain—that the holy name should not be spoken at all and that to do so was blasphemy. Moses' mission as lawgiver and gatherer of Israel was thus preceded by his introduction to the God of Israel.

FEBRUARY 8

I will harden [Pharaoh's] heart,
that he shall not let the people go.
EXODUS 4:21

There are several instances within the book of Exodus and also later in the Old Testament where reference is made to God hardening an individual's heart. An understanding of the doctrine of moral agency, the plan of salvation, and our Father's eagerness to save as many of his children as will be saved shows us that such an idea is foreign to the truth. God does not tempt his children, nor does he harden their hearts. The Joseph Smith Translation of Exodus 4:21 helps us understand that people harden their own hearts, and when they refuse to repent, God permits them to continue in their sinful, habituated course to reap the consequences.

And Pharaoh said, Who is the Lord, that I should obey his voice to let Israel go? I know not the Lord, neither will I let Israel go.

EXODUS 5:2

Surely without realizing it, Pharaoh was repeating the words of the man who is the first son of perdition, even Cain himself (Moses 5:16). Those who know not the Lord know not his majesty and magnificence. Those who know not the Lord know not his power and perpetuity. And those who know not the Lord know not that he rewards those who receive his word and punishes those who reject his word, for he will extend justice to both the faithful and the faithless at the day of judgment. Pharaoh, typical of all natural men, knew only of things pertaining to the natural world. God must be revealed by the power of the Spirit, or he remains forever unknown.

FEBRUARY 10

And I appeared unto Abraham, unto Isaac, and unto Jacob, by the name of God Almighty, but by my name JEHOVAH was I not known to them.

EXODUS 6:3

We have been taught by the prophets that all revelation since the fall of man has come by and through Jehovah, who is Jesus Christ, our Lord and Savior. We know from modern revelation that Jehovah manifested himself to Adam, to Enoch, to Noah, to Abraham, and to the descendants of Abraham. He is the God of the ancients. This verse has caused no small amount of mischief in understanding the God of the Old Testament: Many of the world's great scholars have concluded that the name *Jehovah* was not known until this precise moment on the mountain. Once again the Joseph Smith Translation comes to our rescue, turns a declarative statement into a question, and thereby clarifies that Jehovah had manifest himself to Moses' predecessors, just as he now manifested himself to the lawgiver.

FEBRUARY 11

And Pharaoh hardened his heart at this time also, neither would he let the people go.

EXODUS 8:32

Signs and wonders and miracles do not create faith. They may fan a flame of faith that is already burning, but the miraculous can only reinforce what is already in place, not create it. As we've been taught in modern revelation, "faith cometh not by signs, but signs follow those that believe. Yea, signs come by faith, not by the will of men, nor as they please, but by the will of God" (D&C 63:9–10).

FEBRUARY 12

And they shall take of the blood [of a lamb without blemish], and strike it on the two side posts and on the upper door post of the houses, wherein they shall eat it.

EXODUS 12:7

In Exodus 12 is initiated one of the most significant types and shadows of all of history, the feast of the Passover. Because Pharaoh had continued to reject the obvious manifestations of God's power, a curse came upon the land that threatened the destruction and death of every firstborn child. Deliverance came only to those who placed on their doorposts the blood of a sacrificed unblemished lamb. What a marvelous and resonant symbol this was, a timely and timeless type of the power of deliverance from the angel of death that is to be found only through the protection of the blood of the sinless Lamb of God, even Jesus Christ. Without his atoning sacrifice, we are naked in our sins and inept in our capacity to escape. Through him we have our sins covered—*atone* means "to cover"—and the way ahead made plain. The Lamb slain from the foundation of the world thus becomes our divine Deliverer (Revelation 13:8; Moses 7:47).

FEBRUARY 13

And Moses stretched out his hand over the sea; and the Lord caused the sea to go back by a strong east wind all that night, and made the sea dry land, and the waters were divided.

EXODUS 14:21

The children of Israel found themselves up against a wall of water, as Pharaoh's armies made their way toward them. A slaughter seemed inevitable. What a remarkable feat was the escape of the children of Israel! It has been remembered for millennia as evidence that God preserves his people from destruction if they trust in his omnipotence. And how would Moses know to part the waters of the Red Sea? We learn in a modern revelation: "Yea, behold, I will tell you in your mind and in your heart, by the Holy Ghost, which shall come upon you and which shall dwell in your heart. Now, behold, this is the spirit of revelation; behold, this is the spirit by which Moses brought the children of Israel through the Red Sea on dry ground" (D&C 8:2–3). How did he know? Not by dream. Not by vision. He knew through a manifestation of the Holy Spirit, just as we also may know the will of God.

FEBRUARY 14

The Lord heareth your murmurings which ye murmur against him: and what are we? your murmurings are not against us, but against the Lord.

EXODUS 16:8

We know that the voice of the Lord and the voice of his servants is the same voice; their words are true and shall come to pass (D&C 1:38). We also know that if we receive the word of the Lord through his servants, we are receiving what the Lord would say if he were with us himself (Matthew 10:40). Likewise, when we murmur against the authorized servants of the Lord, we are murmuring against the Lord. We can't have it both ways. If we are disloyal and disobedient to the Lord's representatives in this mortal probation, we are disloyal and disobedient to the Lord. Yes, it is true that, unlike the Lord, those called to positions of leadership are not perfect. We do not believe in prophetic infallibility. Nonetheless, whom the Lord calls, he qualifies. The Lord holds them and each of us accountable for how we follow and serve and submit to the Lord—willingly, humbly, and with full purpose of heart.

FEBRUARY 15

And when the children of Israel saw it, they said one to another, It is manna: for they wist not what it was. And Moses said unto them, This is the bread which the Lord hath given you to eat.
EXODUS 16:15

Most of the time God's miracles address a need through what is available. For example, God provided quails so that the Israelites might have meat. But manna was not something with which they were familiar, not something that was available in their usual environment. The typical Israelite could not have plucked something like it off a tree. Instead, manna (Hebrew, "what is it?") was obviously miraculous. It represented a divine substance that was heavenly and thus literally not of this earth. The miraculous manna met still another need beyond the immediate need of the Israelites for food. It points thoughts, desires, appetites, and affections toward the One who would be the living Bread of Life (John 6:29–56), even the Lord Jesus himself. Jesus was and is the substance that fills our souls and brings us life eternal.

FEBRUARY 16

When Moses held up his hand, . . . Israel prevailed: and when he let down his hand, Amalek prevailed. But Moses' hands were heavy; and they took a stone, and put it under him, and he sat thereon; and Aaron and Hur stayed up his hands.

EXODUS 17:11–12

In our dispensation, sometimes the president of the Church has been a man advanced in years. At times it has been difficult for him to do all he would have liked to do, to travel or to counsel and warn the Saints and the people of the world from his unique perspective. Thus he has needed special helpers—counselors, men of like faith and spiritual aptitude, men filled with the spirit of prophecy and revelation—who hold up his weary arms and sustain him before the people. The counsel came to Frederick G. Williams, a member of the First Presidency, "Wherefore, be faithful; stand in the office which I have appointed unto you; succor the weak, lift up the hands which hang down, and strengthen the feeble knees" (D&C 81:5). Like Aaron and Hur, counselors in the First Presidency assist the president to lead the people of God to victory.

Moses sat to judge the people: and the people stood by Moses from the morning unto the evening. . . . And [Jethro] said unto him, The thing that thou doest is not good. Thou wilt surely wear away, both thou, and this people that is with thee.

EXODUS 18:13–18

Moses loved his people and sought to magnify the calling that God had given to him as the leader of the Israelite nation. But there was a vital lesson Moses (and all others after Moses) needed to learn—namely, no one man can handle it all by himself. Jethro taught Moses the marvelous leadership principle of delegation: "And thou shalt teach them ordinances and laws, and shalt shew them the way wherein they must walk, and the work that they must do" (Exodus 18:20). The Prophet Joseph Smith later voiced the same principle: "I teach them correct principles, and they govern themselves" (in Taylor, *Journal of Discourses,* 10:57–58).

FEBRUARY 18

If ye will obey my voice indeed, and keep my covenant,
then ye shall be a peculiar treasure unto me above all people.

EXODUS 19:5

Exodus 19:5 contains one of the most beautiful promises in all of holy writ, a promise to individuals and nations. God covenants with his people that if we will obey his voice and be true to the gospel covenant, we shall become unto him a "peculiar treasure." The Hebrew word *segullah* refers to a redeemed people and, even more poignantly, to a purchased people. Our peculiarity lies not alone in our speech and our behavior being distinctly different from those of the world but also in the truth that we are not our own, for we have been bought with a price, even the precious blood of Jesus Christ (1 Corinthians 6:19–20; 7:23; 1 Peter 1:18–20; 2:9). In other words, when the Lord of Life returns to "make up [his] jewels" (Malachi 3:17; D&C 60:4; 101:3), he will gather those who have become the sheep of his fold, his precious ones.

FEBRUARY 19

And ye shall be unto me a kingdom of priests, and an holy nation.

EXODUS 19:6

Israel is gathered first to Christ and second to a place: She is gathered to the Lord Jesus Christ, his Church, and his gospel, and then to the lands of her inheritance (or the congregations of the faithful). Baptism is the ordinance that confirms and evidences our faith and repentance and also admits us formally into the house of Israel, where we are gathered to the household of faith. The process of gathering is not complete, however, until we progress spiritually to the point where we are worthy to receive the covenants and ordinances of the holy temple, those divine statutes that prepare men and women to become kings and queens, priests and priestesses unto God in the house of Israel. All other programs and procedures, all other labors in the Church and kingdom, are preparatory to this final stage of gathering.

FEBRUARY 20

Thou shalt have no other gods before me.

EXODUS 20:3

Whereas the ancients too often centered their affections on gods made of wood or stone or metal, idols in our day are more likely to take the form of portfolios, stock options, chrome, size or location of houses, vacations, country clubs, and social circles. Yet anything that entices our hearts or minds away from the sincere worship of the true and living God and the labors associated with the establishment of Zion is an idol. How apt was the Lord's description of the state of the world at the time he called the Choice Seer, Joseph Smith: "They seek not the Lord to establish his righteousness, but every man walketh in his own way, and after the image of his own god" (D&C 1:16). President Ezra Taft Benson taught us that when God is at the top of our list of priorities, all other things either take their proper place beneath him or fall out of the list completely (Conference Report, April 1988, 3).

FEBRUARY 21

Thou shalt not take the name of the Lord thy God in vain; for the Lord will not hold him guiltless that taketh his name in vain.

EXODUS 20:7

Turn on the TV or go to a movie or listen to conversation on any street corner and you will inevitably hear the disrespectful and wholly inappropriate use of the sacred names of Deity. Nevertheless, how we use his name is a matter of grave concern to the Lord—so much so that he included it among his Ten Commandments. Those who profane the name of God have disconnected its sacredness from the majesty of its Source. In ancient days, the irreverent use of the holy name of Deity was a capital offense. Today, such irreverence is so commonplace that, it seems, we are numb to its use. It is a manifestation of a spiritual weakness, an indication that the speaker lacks a richness of expression and the strength of character to use more appropriate words. The Lord through his prophets, ancient and modern, has issued the same command down the centuries: "Thou shalt not take the name of the Lord thy God in vain."

Remember the sabbath day, to keep it holy.
EXODUS 20:8

The commandment to keep the Sabbath holy is an admonishment to God's children that we rest on one day in seven and sanctify the day, commemorative of what he did after six periods of creation. The Lord himself "rested the seventh day: wherefore the Lord blessed the Sabbath day, and hallowed it" (Exodus 20:11). We sanctify and hallow this holy day when we "rest from [our] labors, and pay [our] devotions unto the Most High" (D&C 59:10). On this day we are to set aside temporal things and enjoy more fully the things of eternity. It is a day designed to help us keep unspotted from the world: a day to rest, to serve, to attend Church meetings and partake of the sacrament, to gather as families, to ponder and pray, to renew ourselves spiritually and physically. We thank the Lord for the Sabbath, a day we are to hallow gladly, with thanksgiving and cheerful hearts and countenances (D&C 59:15).

Honour thy father and thy mother: that thy days may be long upon the land which the Lord thy God giveth thee.
EXODUS 20:12

Exodus 20:12 sets forth a commandment, or principle, with a promise: If we show respect and love to our parents and follow their counsel, our days will be lengthened and our nation will be preserved. Surely the sobering converse is equally true: a nation in which children are disrespectful to parents, shun parental advice, and reject time-honored moral values is on the high road to apostasy, traveling toward destruction by the most direct route. It is significant that the apostle Paul, in writing of the perils of the last days, predicted: "For men shall be lovers of their own selves, covetous, boasters, proud, blasphemers, *disobedient to parents,* unthankful, unholy, without natural affection" (2 Timothy 3:2–3; emphasis added). A society of the pure in heart is made up of individuals who do good and avoid evil, not merely because doing good is the right thing to do but also because doing so brings honor and respect to those who taught them so to do.

Thou shalt not kill.

EXODUS 20:13

The word translated here as "kill" refers to willful, premeditated murder. There are some things over which we do not have control, some things which are beyond our reach, some things that are better left alone, some things that must be kept within proper bounds. One of these is life. Because God is the giver of life, he is the one who knows when it is appropriate for life to come forth and when it is appropriate for life to be taken. That is why murder committed by one who walks in the light of gospel understanding is considered an unforgivable sin (Smith, *Teachings,* 339). Surely anticipating our day, a time when countless millions of the unborn whose opportunity for mortality has been postponed through the hideous crime of abortion, the Lord said: "Thou shalt . . . not kill, nor do anything like unto it" (D&C 59:6). Life is precious. We must do all in our power to encourage it and preserve it.

FEBRUARY 25

Thou shalt not commit adultery.

EXODUS 20:14

Sins against the law of chastity are extremely serious for many reasons. First, as with murder, violations of the law of chastity tamper with the very powers of life. Second, once taken, virtue cannot be restored. Third, immorality spawns a whole host of fellow travelers: feelings of inadequacy, feelings of betrayal, feelings of jealousy, a loss of hope, and so on. Finally, immorality is closely associated with the violation of two other commandments—the command against lying (Exodus 20:16) and the command against coveting that which is not our own (Exodus 20:17). History teaches us the sobering lesson that nations who have allowed their moral standards to decline to the point where immorality prevails are nations that crumble eventually beneath the weight of their own iniquity.

Thou shalt not steal.

EXODUS 20:15

In the premortal realm, Lucifer, motivated by pride, wanted to steal the Father's plan and glory to bring honor unto himself. From Satan to Cain and on through today, all who steal want something for nothing. They seek self-aggrandizement through stolen power, prestige, or possessions. But Father's plan of happiness for his children provides no shortcuts or end runs around immutable law and timeless principles. When we keep the commandments and fully do our part to live truthfully, the Lord will reward us with strength for the journey of life and everlasting joy hereafter (D&C 130:20–21). We are to be people of honesty and honor, people of veracity and virtue. Refraining from stealing is much more than merely refraining from taking things from someone else. We are to exemplify in our lives "a more excellent way" (Ether 12:11) in our manner of thought and action: We are to manifest honor to the God who made us by walking with integrity and truth.

FEBRUARY 27

Thus shalt not bear false witness against thy neighbour.

EXODUS 20:16

It is sad that many often believe the worst and condemn quickly, often based on nothing more than something someone else has said or done or seen. People who have made up their minds to find fault, spread stories, and "make a man an offender for a word" (Isaiah 29:21) seldom see the good in others. To bear witness and make judgments based on gossip or emotion or appearance or malevolence or immaturity is a kind of character assassination that is unworthy of us all. "Judge not according to the appearance," said Jesus, "but judge righteous judgment" (John 7:24). "For with what judgment ye judge, ye shall be judged: and with what measure ye mete, it shall be measured to you again" (Matthew 7:2). We all make mistakes. We all need patience, understanding, and forgiveness. To hold our tongue, to refuse to savor rumors and gossip or spread lies or half-truths about another, requires the self-discipline and the abundant heart of a true disciple of Christ.

Thou shalt not covet.

EXODUS 20:17

The last of the Ten Commandments admonishes us not to lust after that which is not our own—"thy neighbour's house . . . thy neighbour's wife, nor his manservant, nor his maidservant, nor his ox, nor his ass, nor any thing that is thy neighbor's" (Exodus 20:17). Elder Jeffrey R. Holland said, "Most 'thou shalt not' commandments are meant to keep us from hurting others, but I am convinced the commandment not 'to covet' is meant to keep us from hurting ourselves" (*Ensign,* May 2002, 64). We die a slow spiritual death as we covet; we are halted in our progression as we yearn for possessions and prestige that others may enjoy; we hurt ourselves here and hereafter, for when we covet, we cannot feel "the peace which passeth understanding" (Philippians 4:7). Hearts full of envy can never be right with the Lord.

MARCH

For the life of the flesh is in the blood:
and I have given it to you upon the altar
to make an atonement for your souls.
LEVITICUS 17:11

MARCH 1

And they said unto Moses, Speak thou with us,
and we will hear: but let not God speak with us, lest we die.
EXODUS 20:19

Exodus 20:19 is a haunting and tragic passage that bespeaks a people who wanted to enjoy the blessings of God—but not fully. They were thrilled to see the holy cloud that represented the presence of Jehovah resting over their tabernacle, but they were not anxious to enter the immediate presence of the Almighty. The Melchizedek Priesthood makes available the power of godliness, without which "no man can see the face of God, even the Father, and live. Now this Moses plainly taught to the children of Israel in the wilderness, and sought diligently to sanctify his people that they might behold the face of God; but they hardened their hearts and could not endure his presence" (D&C 84:21–24). Thus this generation of the children of Israel were not allowed to enter the promised land: They were not prepared to receive the fulness of the blessings of the Melchizedek Priesthood or to enjoy the association of Moses, the man who held those keys in their fulness.

MARCH 2

Wherefore the children of Israel shall keep the sabbath . . . for a perpetual covenant. It is a sign between me and the children of Israel for ever: for in six days the Lord made heaven and earth, and on the seventh day he rested, and was refreshed.

EXODUS 31:16–17

Keeping the Sabbath holy is an outward manifestation of an inner commitment to follow the Lord. The Sabbath was established to commemorate God's day of rest after the Creation (Ephesians 20:10–11) and Israel's redemption from Egyptian captivity (Deuteronomy 5:15). The Lord said to Moses, "Verily my Sabbaths ye shall keep: for it is a sign between me and you throughout your generations; that ye may know that I am the Lord that doth sanctify you" (Exodus 31:13). The Sabbath is a constant reminder, a perpetual covenant, an eternal principle that existed from the days of Adam. It is a day to separate ourselves more fully from the world, a day to be spiritually strengthened, a day to gather with the Saints in worship, a day to serve others and do our duty to God, a day to rest and receive heavenly help for the week ahead. Perhaps now more than ever, we need the spiritual sustenance that comes from sincere observance of the Sabbath.

MARCH 3

When the people saw that Moses delayed to come down out of the mount, the people gathered themselves together unto Aaron, and said unto him, Up, make us gods, which shall go before us; for as for this Moses . . . we wot not what is become of him.

EXODUS 32:1

How easy it was for the ancient Israelites to wander from the path of righteousness in the short time their prophet-leader was on the mount communing with Jehovah. The noble Aaron, an otherwise faithful and obedient servant of the Lord, yielded to the persuasions of a people who had lived for four hundred years in a land steeped in idolatry. It has often been said, and rightly so, that it is one thing to take Israel out of Egypt and quite another to take Egypt out of Israel. It must have been tremendous pressure, but Aaron sinned: He made for the people a molten calf that the people might worship, when not long before the true and living God had given strict instructions against such practices (Exodus 20:3–5). Vigilance and a constant reminder of the commandments of God are forever necessary to avoid the golden calves that beckon for our attention.

MARCH 4

And the Lord spake unto Moses face to face, as a man speaketh unto his friend. And he said, Thou canst not see my face: for there shall no man see me, and live.

EXODUS 33:11, 20

One of the grand and glorious principles restored to the earth through the Prophet Joseph Smith is that our God is knowable and approachable and that eventually the faithful can see his face and know that he is (D&C 93:1; 101:38). In these two verses we see what appears to be a contradiction: Moses sees God face to face, and yet we are told that no man can see God. Such contradictions bespeak the doctrinal errors that entered into the faith and teachings of many who sought to do right but labored without the light of gospel fulness. Either Moses saw God face to face, or he did not. Joseph Smith's translation of the Bible assists us in our understanding: No sinful man can see the face of the Lord and live (JST Exodus 33:20; D&C 67:10–13). God wants his children to learn of him, to come unto him, and one day to stand with confidence in his presence.

MARCH 5

And the Lord said unto Moses, Hew thee two tables of stone like unto the first: and I will write upon these tables the words that were in the first tables, which thou brakest.

EXODUS 34:1

When Moses descended the mountain and discovered that his people had descended into immorality and perversion, he was filled with righteous indignation. Jehovah had revealed to Moses the doctrines, principles, and ordinances associated with the fulness of the everlasting gospel, including the blessings of the temple. But clearly the Israelites were not prepared for such lofty teachings and were unable in their present condition to live saintly lives. Consequently, Moses the lawgiver broke the tablets of stone. God then instructed Moses to prepare a second set of tablets on which God's holy order and ordinances were replaced by what we know as the law of Moses, or the law of carnal commandments (JST Exodus 34:1–2; JST Deuteronomy 10:2; D&C 84:23–27). The Israelites for the next millennium and a half would live by "a law of performances and of ordinances, a law which they were to observe strictly from day to day" (Mosiah 13:30).

Sanctify yourselves, and ye shall be holy; . . . for I am the Lord that bringeth you up out of the land of Egypt, to be your God: ye shall therefore be holy, for I am holy.

LEVITICUS 11:44–45

As Latter-day Saints we strive to live a life that is different, one characterized by complete integrity, moral purity, and charity. In short, we are called to live a holy life. We, as "followers of God" (Ephesians 5:1), are to follow the Perfect Model, living as he lives. It takes time to grow spiritually. We cannot cram or take shortcuts to the life of righteousness. It takes time to cultivate a way of walking with the Lord that comes naturally because the enemy within (natural man) has been subdued. It takes time to be holy, to turn our thoughts and feelings heavenward, to reflect the gospel in our actions and attitudes. The Lord will help us. Just as he rescued ancient Israel, he will rescue us. We must turn to him to cleanse our thoughts, to correct our proud ways, to forgive us completely, and to make us holy vessels who bring glory to his name. God has called us to be holy.

MARCH 7

And the leper in whom the plague is, his clothes shall be rent, and his head bare, . . . and shall cry, Unclean, unclean.
LEVITICUS 13:45

Those suffering with leprosy in the time of Jesus were required to cover their faces and cry out "unclean, unclean" when approaching others not so afflicted. Theirs was a warning to stay away from leprosy's living death. Today, our faces may hide a type of spiritual leprosy—we safeguard our sins and wrongdoings, we hide our fleshly susceptibilities and weaknesses so that others do not know that we are unclean. But to one extent or another, we are all unclean. "All have sinned, and come short of the glory of God," said the apostle Paul (Romans 3:23). We all need the merciful rescue and cleansing grace of the Lord. Without the Savior's gracious and loving atonement, we are forever lost and unclean. We cry out like the lepers of old, "Jesus, Master, have mercy on us" (Luke 17:13). Our only hope, the only cure for our spiritual malady, is to seek the Atoning One. In Jesus we will find rest to our souls (Matthew 11:29).

MARCH 8

For the life of the flesh is in the blood: and I have given it to you upon the altar to make an atonement for your souls: for it is the blood that maketh an atonement for the soul.

LEVITICUS 17:11

Clearly, blood has a dual meaning: it is the emblem of mortality, that which each human possesses while living on earth and that which keeps us alive for a short season, but eventually it is that which is the means by which we decay and die. Blood is also the emblem of immortality and eternal life, for it is through the shedding of the precious blood of Christ that each of us is able to put off the natural man, have our souls cleansed and purified, and become holy under the direction of the Holy One of Israel. As Paul taught so clearly to the early Saints, it is not simply the blood of sacrificial animals which brought remission of sins (Hebrews 10:4), but rather the blood of the great and last sacrifice, even the Son of God. One does not exercise faith in an animal, but rather in that which the animal typified. Truly, there is power in the blood!

MARCH 9

Ye shall not steal, neither deal falsely, neither lie one to another.

LEVITICUS 19:11

Dishonesty is dangerous to spiritual and physical health, psychological well-being, and personal relationships. It is a snare, a self-built jail that puts us in bondage to hypocrisy, deceit, and pretense. It is an accomplice to every sin. The thought that we can win by cheating, stealing, and lying *is* a lie. The prophet Alma asks us to imagine ourselves at the judgment bar of God: "Do ye imagine to yourselves that ye can lie unto the Lord in that day, and say—Lord, our works have been righteous works upon the face of the earth—and that he will save you?" (Alma 5:17). We cannot lie our way to eternal life; we cannot steal heaven; we cannot cheat our way into glory. We must be people of impeccable honesty and integrity, people who not only believe truth but live truthfully.

MARCH 10

Thou shalt not avenge, nor bear any grudge against the children of thy people, but thou shalt love thy neighbour as thyself: I am the Lord.

LEVITICUS 19:18

The premortal Messiah quoted his own Mosaic law when he said, "Thou shalt love thy neighbor as thyself" (Leviticus 19:18). Later, he taught the people of the meridian dispensation, "Thou shalt love the Lord thy God will all thy heart, and with all thy soul, and with all thy mind. This is the first and great commandment. And the second is like unto it, Thou shalt love thy neighbour as thyself. On these two commandments hang all the law and the prophets" (Matthew 22:37–40). If we truly love God, we will genuinely love others. The Lord commands in our day, "Exalt not yourselves" and "Thou shalt not be proud in thy heart" (D&C 112:15; 42:40). He asks us to be gentle, humble, unassertive enough to turn the other cheek, long-suffering, meek, and lowly of heart. We are to treat others at least as well as we treat ourselves—with kindness and charity. We are expected to love God and all others.

But the stranger that dwelleth with you shall be unto you as one born among you, and thou shalt love him as thyself; for ye were strangers in the land of Egypt: I am the Lord your God.
LEVITICUS 19:34

If you've ever traveled to an unfamiliar place and felt like a stranger, you know how wonderful it feels to be welcomed and made to feel at home. As people join the Church or move into our ward or branch, we can extend the hand of friendship and reach out in love and compassion. The truth is that we are all "strangers" to this fallen world—away from our heavenly home for a season. We all have a universal need to feel that there are caring people around us who are concerned about us and have our best interests at heart. New members of the Church need a friend; new neighbors need a warm welcome; all people in our homes and communities need the reassurance of continuing friendship. We need the understanding and empathy manifest in living the Golden Rule—treating others the way we wish to be treated: "Whatsoever ye would that men should do to you, do ye even so to them," taught the Savior (Matthew 7:12).

MARCH 12

Sanctify yourselves therefore, and be ye holy: for I am the Lord your God.
LEVITICUS 20:7

The fundamental gospel message is that we can repent and become new creatures in Christ. We live in a world filled with temptation, a world difficult to overcome—and we all fall short of perfection. President Gordon B. Hinckley said, "I wish to emphasize that if you make a mistake, it can be forgiven, it can be overcome, it can be lived above. You can go on to success and happiness. But I hope that such an experience will not come your way, and I am confident it will not if you will set your mind and pray for the strength to walk the high road, which at times may be lonely but which will lead to peace and happiness and joy supernal in this life and everlastingly hereafter" (*Ensign,* May 2004, 115). We are sanctified—made clean, holy, and pure through the blood of Christ by the medium of the Holy Ghost—gradually, line upon line.

MARCH 13

The Lord bless thee, and keep thee: The Lord make his face shine upon thee, and be gracious unto thee: The Lord lift up his countenance upon thee, and give thee peace.

NUMBERS 6:24–26

The last verses of Numbers 6 record a beautiful priesthood blessing for Israel. Its words have been used by ministers of various faiths for generations, and they have been set to music and sung by choirs around the world. The supplication is for the Lord to watch over his children, to pour out his promised blessings upon true disciples, to grant us peace as he puts his name upon us (Numbers 6:27). We become the sons and daughters of Christ through faithful covenant keeping. Said King Benjamin, "And now, because of the covenant which ye have made ye shall be called the children of Christ, his sons, and his daughters; for behold, this day he hath spiritually begotten you; for ye say that your hearts are changed through faith on his name . . . I would that ye should remember to retain the name written always in your hearts" (Mosiah 5:7–12). As we keep our covenants, the Lord will bless and keep us.

MARCH 14

Would God that all the Lord's people were prophets, and that the Lord would put his spirit upon them!

NUMBERS 11:29

Each of us is a prophet to the extent that we have a testimony of the risen Lord. The apostle Paul said, "No man can say that Jesus is the Lord, but by the Holy Ghost" (1 Corinthians 12:3). And John the Revelator added his witness: "The testimony of Jesus is the spirit of prophecy" (Revelation 19:10). We partake of the prophetic gift as we nurture a testimony of Jesus and as we bear witness of our Lord. We are to seek the Spirit in our lives and be guided by its inspiration. Any revelatory prompting we receive will be for our area of stewardship and in accord with the scriptures and the words of the ordained apostles and prophets. The gift of revelation and the spirit of prophecy are to know that the Lord lives, that we are sons and daughters of God, that the true Church has been restored to the earth, and that the Spirit will whisper truth to our souls.

MARCH 15

If there be a prophet among you, I the Lord will make myself known unto him. . . . With [Moses] will I speak mouth to mouth, even apparently, and not in dark speeches; . . . wherefore then were ye not afraid to speak against my servant Moses?

NUMBERS 12:6–8

Aaron and Miriam began to murmur and criticize their younger brother, Moses. It is clear from their criticisms that their motives were impure, that they were concerned that they were not receiving the public acclaim that Moses was receiving. Jehovah stepped into the conversation suddenly, chastened them dramatically, and then taught a great lesson concerning his covenant spokesmen. In short, he said there are prophets, and then there are prophets! Those like Moses, who are called to stand as dispensation heads, become the preeminent prophetic revealers of Christ and the plan of salvation, the means through which God restores knowledge and perspective and power. Subsequent prophets during a given dispensation are themselves noble and great, but each of them recognizes the singular and significant place of the head of their dispensation.

MARCH 16

The land, which we passed through to search it, is an exceeding good land. If the Lord delight in us, then he will bring us into this land. . . . Only rebel not ye against the Lord, neither fear ye the people of the land . . . the Lord is with us: fear them not.

NUMBERS 14:7–9

Representatives from each of the twelve tribes were sent on a special expedition to determine the challenges they would face and the benefits they would derive from conquering the people of the land. Ten of the twelve spies returned with glowing reports of bounties to be found in the land but that the people living in the land were many, mighty, and unconquerable. Joshua and Caleb returned with a similar positive report about a land flowing with milk and honey, but they, trusting fully in the power of the Almighty to empower the Israelites, strongly recommended that they move in and take the land. The ten spies may have been realistic, but they were faithless. Joshua and Caleb were quick to remember how the God of the ancients had performed miracle after miracle to bring them to where they were now; why could he not assist them in conquering their enemies? In short, Joshua and Caleb refused to take counsel from their fears.

MARCH 17

And they fell upon their faces, and said,
O God, the God of the spirits of all flesh.
Numbers 16:22

As powerful and true to life as are the stories and teachings of the Old Testament, clearly, as explained by the angel to Nephi, many plain and precious truths have been removed from the Holy Bible (1 Nephi 13:20–29). Unfortunately, one of the vital and most central of all deletions from the Old Testament is a full and correct understanding of the nature of God and the Godhead. Missing from the stick of Judah are sacred truths about the three personages within the Divine Presidency, distinctions between the Father and the Son, and the role of the Holy Ghost as a member of that Godhead. Thankfully, there are scriptural allusions here and there which, through the assistance of modern revelation, we are able to appreciate and grasp. God is our Heavenly Father, the Father of the spirits of all men and women, as the New Testament also mentions (Hebrews 12:9).

MARCH 18

And the Lord said unto Moses, Make thee a fiery serpent, and set it upon a pole: and it shall come to pass, that every one that is bitten, when he looketh upon it, shall live.
NUMBERS 21:8

The Lord sent fiery flying serpents among ancient Israel to straiten and humble them, "and after they were bitten [the Lord] prepared a way that they might be healed; and the labor which they had to perform was to look; and because of the simpleness of the way, or the easiness of it, there were many who perished" (1 Nephi 17:41). Sadly, many had become so hardened because of their disbelief, so blind to truth, that they would not look (Alma 33:19–21). It was too easy, too simple, too silly to look at a brass serpent on a pole and expect to live. But the Lord's words were fulfilled: "And Moses made a serpent of brass, and put it upon a pole, and it came to pass, that if a serpent had bitten any man, when he beheld the serpent of brass, he lived" (Numbers 21:9). Abundant blessings come to those who follow the Lord and his prophet in all things.

MARCH 19

If a man vow a vow unto the Lord . . . he shall not break his word, he shall do according to all that proceedeth out of his mouth.
NUMBERS 30:2

Those with integrity of heart live so that what they believe is reflected in who they are: how they think, act, and interact. Their word is their bond, and what they say they'll do, they do. When we have integrity, not only do we choose the right but we choose it for the right reasons. We act out of love rather than for outward appearance. We uphold sacred truths, regardless of setting or circumstance. If we make a covenant with the Lord, we follow through and stay committed and faithful. If we give our word to any person, we do our very best to keep our word and be dependable and honest. Living truthfully invites deep trust, abiding love, and inner peace. It fuses right actions with pure motives. And although we all make mistakes and fall short, those with integrity of heart are teachable and humble because they "[love] that which is right" (D&C 124:15). They strive each day with all their hearts to live truthfully.

But if from thence thou shalt seek the Lord thy God, thou shalt find him, if thou seek him with all thy heart and with all thy soul.

DEUTERONOMY 4:29

God's love for us, his children, is perfect, constant, and never ending. He stands ready to receive us as we seek him with full purpose of heart. James counseled in his epistle: "Submit yourselves therefore to God. Resist the devil, and he will flee from you. Draw nigh to God, and he will draw nigh to you. Cleanse your hands, ye sinners; and purify your hearts, ye double minded" (James 4:7–8). There we have the formula to find rest in the Lord: Submit ourselves in humility and meekness as we recognize our complete dependence upon him; stand firm against the mighty winds of the adversary by building upon the sure foundation of the Redeemer (Helaman 5:12); diligently seek the Lord through scripture study, pondering, and praying; and purifying our hearts by drawing upon the power of the infinite atonement through repentance and forgiveness. He stands at the door and knocks; we must open the door (Revelation 3:20).

MARCH 21

When thou art in tribulation . . . if thou turn to the Lord thy God, and shalt be obedient unto his voice . . . he will not forsake thee, neither destroy thee, nor forget the covenant of thy fathers.

DEUTERONOMY 4:30–31

Israel is scattered in wickedness and apostasy when it worships the gods of this world. But in the latter day—our day—Israel will once again be gathered as people seek the Lord and his righteousness and enter into covenants with him. As we turn to the Lord with all our heart, he will bless and inspire us. As we are obedient and faithful to the gospel, the Lord's words of eternal life, he will ever comfort and direct us. "Draw near unto me and I will draw near unto you; seek me diligently and ye shall find me; ask, and ye shall receive; knock, and it shall be opened unto you" (D&C 88:63). The Lord is bound by everlasting covenant when we do what he says; but when we disobey because of pride and sinfulness and worldly preoccupation, we have no promise (D&C 82:10). To enter into the joy and peace of the Lord, we must turn to him.

MARCH 22

Know therefore this day, and consider it in thine heart, that the Lord he is God in heaven above, and upon the earth beneath: there is none else.

DEUTERONOMY 4:39

The greatest truth one can possess is the knowledge that God is in his heaven and we are his beloved sons and daughters. In the inspired words of King Benjamin, "Believe in God; believe that he is, and that he created all things, both in heaven and in earth; believe that he has all wisdom, and all power, both in heaven and in earth; believe that man doth not comprehend all the things which the Lord can comprehend" (Mosiah 4:9). But we must have a correct understanding of who God is. True, he is above all things; he is all-powerful and all-knowing. But he is also our Heavenly Father, our loving and long-suffering Father. His Son is our Redeemer, our elder and merciful Brother. When we have a deep and abiding testimony of these fundamental truths about the nature and character of the Father and Son, we begin to comprehend our inherent potential and divine possibilities.

MARCH 23

Ye shall observe to do therefore as the Lord your God hath commanded you: ye shall not turn aside to the right hand or to the left.

DEUTERONOMY 5:32

The prophet Moses was one of history's greatest men. His greatness, meekness, and faithfulness in leading ancient Israel out of captivity continues to amaze and inspire us today. His was a divine calling, a ministry of destiny. Always, he pleaded with his people to honor the Lord and observe His commandments: "Ye shall walk in all the ways which the Lord your God hath commanded you, that ye may live, and that it may be well with you, and that ye may prolong your days in the land which ye shall possess" (Deuteronomy 5:33). With the feelings of both a tender parent and a fearless leader, Moses knew that blessings flow from obedience. But he could only encourage, exhort, and prepare his people to enter the promised land. He, like our Lord, would not force faithfulness. We can choose to enjoy our days in mortality in freedom and happiness, or we can be in bondage to sin and murmuring. Let us follow the Lord and live.

Hear, O Israel: The Lord our God is one Lord.

DEUTERONOMY 6:4

Deuteronomy 6:4, one of the most often quoted passages in the entire Old Testament, is called the Shema, from the Hebrew word meaning "hear." For millennia it has been the scriptural basis for monotheism—the belief in one God—that is held by Judaism, Christianity, and Islam. To be sure, there are three personages in the Godhead, and each of these personages possesses all of the godly attributes in perfection. They are so completely united in thought, word, purpose, will, mind, and power—indeed, they are infinitely more one than separate—that they are occasionally referred to collectively, even in the Book of Mormon, as God (2 Nephi 31:21; Alma 11:44; Mormon 7:7). The Prophet Joseph Smith brought clarity to what seemed to him to be confusion in the creeds of Christendom when he emphasized that the Godhead consists of "three distinct personages and three Gods" (*Teachings*, 370), while affirming the unity of the Godhead.

MARCH 25

And thou shalt teach them diligently unto thy children, and shalt talk of them when thou sittest in thine house, and when thou walkest by the way, and when thou liest down, and when thou risest up.

DEUTERONOMY 6:7

The time with our children passes so quickly. Our babies are soon riding bikes, and then driving cars, and before we know it, leaving home. All the while we influence them: We communicate values and establish patterns for them to follow. One generation passes to the next a method of living, a way of relating, a desire for learning, a model of faith. Of course, children may adjust those patterns in their own adult lives. Oftentimes they improve upon family patterns. Yet sometimes they choose a rocky path as they reject virtues their parents hold dear. But even then, when truth has been taught from their youth, they have a map to bring them home. Our responsibility as parents is to lovingly share with our children what is sacred to us. We must live our beliefs. By precept and example, we must let our children know what we believe. We must let them feel our love for them and for the God who made them.

MARCH 26

Then beware lest thou forget the Lord, which brought thee forth out of the land of Egypt, from the house of bondage.
DEUTERONOMY 6:12

One of the most important words in the dictionary is the word *remember* (Kimball, *Circles of Exaltation,* 8). How often do we stray from the strait path because we forget who we are and Whose we are? How often do we fall into temptation because we forget that some present pleasures lead only to heartache hereafter? And how often do we forget the price that has been paid by so many noble men and women to bring to us the knowledge and understanding we possess, persons who gave their very lives to lay the foundation of this great latter-day work? If we are sensitive, attentive to the quiet whisperings of the spirit of conscience within us, we will remember and be tutored through the medium of memory.

MARCH 27

For thou art an holy people unto the Lord thy God: the Lord thy God hath chosen thee to be a special people unto himself, above all people that are upon the face of the earth.

DEUTERONOMY 7:6

It is not easy in a day of widening wickedness and spreading secularity to focus ourselves upon a life of holiness. To be holy is to be whole, complete, mature, and riveted on the Lord and on things of righteousness. A holy person withdraws not from society but from the sins of society. A holy person does not preach from the tower of self-righteousness but instead entices others to be their very best through the power of a noble example. The Saints of the Most High are, of course, called upon to keep the Sabbath day holy (Exodus 20:8) but are further commissioned to do all they can to keep every day holy (D&C 59:11), to search out and embody the good, and to eschew the evil and vain things of the world. In the words of the Savior, they are called upon to be "the light of the world" (Matthew 5:14), to make a difference by being different.

MARCH 28

And thou shalt remember all the way which the Lord thy God led thee these forty years in the wilderness, to humble thee, and to prove thee, to know what was in thine heart.

DEUTERONOMY 8:2

This life is full of "wilderness experiences" that test our mettle and provide opportunities to soften our hearts. Indeed, our hearts are revealed in the crucibles of suffering. We can become bitter and angry because of tribulations, or we can become stronger, more faithful, and humble. These divine tutorials are preparing us for eternal life hereafter, even as they expand our souls in mortality. We can develop the attributes of godliness in the furnace of affliction. We can prove ourselves worthy of exaltation. In life's journey, the Lord will not leave us comfortless. As he did for ancient Israel, the Lord will lead us, guide us, and walk beside us (*Hymns,* no. 301). If we stay on the path and strive for righteousness with all our hearts despite mistakes and shortcomings, he will not abandon us or forsake us. His promise is sure.

MARCH 29

What doth the Lord thy God require of thee, but to fear the Lord thy God, to walk in all his ways, and to love him, and to serve the Lord thy God with all thy heart.

DEUTERONOMY 10:12

When Moses came down from the mount after forty days and forty nights, he carried with him both the law and a greater understanding of the Lord. Moses summarized the tables of stone containing the Ten Commandments when he told the people what the Lord required of them: to respect the Lord God, to keep his commandments, to love him, to serve him with heart and soul. In the meridian dispensation, the Lord said simply, "If ye love me, keep my commandments" (John 14:15). The clearest manifestation of our love for God is our diligence in serving him and keeping his commandments. True disciples of Christ do not obey out of fear, or pride, or hope of self-aggrandizement. The truly converted obey because they love Heavenly Father and Jesus. They wish to become like them and inherit eternal life.

I set before you this day a blessing and a curse; a blessing, if ye obey the commandments of the Lord your God . . . : and a curse, if ye will not obey . . . , but turn aside out of the way which I command you this day, to go after other gods.
DEUTERONOMY 11:26–28

Deuteronomy 11:26–28 embodies what has come to be known as the Deuteronomic Code—the simple, straightforward, black-and-white principle of keeping or breaking the commandments of the Almighty (also Deuteronomy 30:15–20). It is a code that is followed by the writers of the Book of Mormon, one that holds up before our eyes the stark and simple reality that faithfully observing the statutes and laws of God leads to an enjoyment of his blessings; breaking his laws leads to the curse of losing his Spirit, his favor, and the feelings associated with the sweet support of his sustaining love.

MARCH 31

Every man shall give as he is able, according to the blessing of the Lord thy God which he hath given thee.

DEUTERONOMY 16:17

What we willingly give is less a measure of our bank accounts than it is a measure of our hearts. The poor widow cast into the treasury her last two mites (Mark 12:42–44), and another widow shared her last meal with Elijah (1 Kings 17:9–16). King Benjamin asked: "Are we not all beggars? Do we not all depend upon the same Being, even God, for all the substance which we have . . . ?" (Mosiah 4:19). We have been given much; we too must give (*Hymns,* no. 219). For those with little, King Benjamin taught, "I would that ye say in your hearts that: I give not because I have not, but if I had I would give" (Mosiah 4:24). From the abundance of our hearts, we offer our time, our willingness, our kindness and goodness to others. The Savior's teaching on earthly and heavenly treasures offers everlasting truth: "For where your treasure is, there will your heart be also" (Matthew 6:21).

APRIL

Would God that all the Lord's people were prophets, and that the Lord would put his spirit upon them!

NUMBERS 11:29

APRIL 1

And he shall read therein all the days of his life: that he may learn to fear the Lord his God, to keep all the words of this law and these statutes, to do them.

DEUTERONOMY 17:19

Scriptures contain the word of God; they are the "true scripts" that we can trust to stand the test of time. They contain the warnings and doctrinal teachings of those who were moved upon by the Holy Ghost and thus spoke with the tongues of angels (2 Nephi 32:3; 33:10). As we study the scriptures, we are instructed in everlasting things; we become spiritually strengthened and deepen our resolve to respect the Lord by keeping his commandments. We can draw parallels to our own lives as we "liken all scriptures unto us, that it might be for our profit and learning" (1 Nephi 19:23). To read and ponder them is to hear the voice of the Master (D&C 18:34–36). Those who cherish and are grounded in the scriptures are better able to distinguish the divine from the devilish, the sacred from the secular. What a remarkable blessing and privilege it is to daily feast upon the words of eternal life found in the scriptures.

APRIL 2

The Lord thy God will raise up unto thee a Prophet from the midst of thee, of thy brethren, like unto me; unto him ye shall hearken. [I] will put my words in his mouth; and he shall speak unto them all that I shall command him.

DEUTERONOMY 18:15, 18

Jesus Christ, our Savior and Redeemer, is the Promised Messiah, the Anointed One. He is the great "High Priest of our profession," the King of kings and Lord of lords (Hebrews 3:1). In addition, Jesus was a prophet; indeed, he was and is the Prophet above all other prophets. Jehovah declares that God would in the future raise up a Prophet like unto Moses, in truth, the Lawgiver of all lawgivers, the One whom Moses worshiped and of whom he was a type and a shadow (Joseph Smith–History 1:40).

APRIL 3

I have set before you life and death, blessing and cursing: therefore choose life.

DEUTERONOMY 30:19

Our greatest endowment is the freedom to choose. Agency, the ability to choose our life and what we'll be, is the foundation of the Father's great plan of happiness. The Lord and his gospel dictate no compulsion or manipulation in our soul freedom. We can choose the life and liberty that come of righteous choices, or we can choose the burden and slavery of sin. Samuel the Lamanite declared, "Ye are free; ye are permitted to act for yourselves; for behold, God hath given unto you a knowledge and he hath made you free. . . . and he hath given unto you that ye might choose life or death" (Helaman 14:30–31). We can choose the life that comes of following the Savior and become alive in him (2 Nephi 25:25). We can choose a life of willing submission to the Lord, which will grant us victory over the trials and temptations of life (D&C 104:82). We are free to choose.

APRIL 4

When the most High divided to the nations their inheritance, when he separated the sons of Adam, he set the bounds of the people according to the number of the children of Israel. For the Lord's portion is his people; Jacob is the lot of his inheritance.

DEUTERONOMY 32:8–9

How, when, and under what circumstances we come to earth are no accident. Our Heavenly Father has a divine plan, a timetable, a sacred scheme, by which his spirit sons and daughters come into their second estate. One factor governing the placement of individuals on earth is linked to the election of the house of Israel. Persons who were true and faithful in their first estate come into mortality as a part of this predesigned program by which they may have a leavening influence among all the children of God. Jehovah's promise to Abraham that his posterity would prove a blessing to all humankind is thereby fulfilled.

APRIL 5

His glory is like the firstling of his bullock, and his horns are like the horns of unicorns: with them he shall push the people together to the ends of the earth: and they are the ten thousands of Ephraim, and they are the thousands of Manasseh.

DEUTERONOMY 33:17

Surely no work is more significant than the work of gathering Israel, the process by which persons hear and receive the message of salvation, repent of their sins, are baptized and confirmed by proper authority, receive the blessings of the temple, congregate with the Saints, and endure faithfully until the end of their lives. Although all of Abraham's descendants who have come unto the true fold of God are charged to invite others to come unto Christ, the keys or directing power associated with the gathering are held by the tribe of Joseph, the birthright tribe. Ephraim and Manasseh are here commissioned to "push the people together from the ends of the earth" (D&C 58:45), to direct missionary work of the Church of Jesus Christ, and to see to the retention of those who have been converted.

APRIL 6

So Moses the servant of the Lord died there in the land of Moab, according to the word of the Lord. And he buried him in a valley in the land of Moab, over against Beth-peor: but no man knoweth of his sepulchre unto this day.

DEUTERONOMY 34:5–6

Deuteronomy 34:5–6 is a place in the Bible from which precious truths have been lost. Moses did not die in Moab; rather, he was translated, taken into heaven without tasting death. Others, including Melchizedek, Alma the Younger (Alma 45:18–19), and the people of Enoch, were similarly translated. Translated beings are given special assignments to minister in behalf of their Lord (Smith, *Teachings,* 170–71, 191). Moses retained his physical body so that he might appear on the Mount of Transfiguration with other prophetic colleagues to confer the keys of the kingdom upon Peter, James, and John (Matthew 17:1–8; Smith, *Teachings,* 158). As with all the others who were translated before the resurrection of Christ, Moses went through an instantaneous death and resurrection after our Lord's rise from the tomb (D&C 133:54–55). Moses returned to the earth on 3 April 1836 to confer upon Joseph Smith and Oliver Cowdery the keys of the gathering of Israel (D&C 110:11).

APRIL 7

As I was with Moses, so I will be with thee: I will not fail thee, nor forsake thee. Be strong and of a good courage: for unto this people shalt thou divide for an inheritance the land, which I sware unto their fathers to give them.

JOSHUA 1:5–6

Our all-wise and all-loving Father in heaven knows what is best for his children and who should lead them at any given period of time. It is hard to imagine a prophet-leader who could have been more loved and revered by the children of Israel than Moses. And yet when Moses' ministry on earth was finished, Jehovah called upon Joshua to stand as the new prophet and seer. Joshua must have felt an overwhelming sense of inadequacy as he contemplated standing in Moses' shoes, but the Lord did not want Joshua to be Moses—he wanted Joshua to be Joshua. The marvelous passage in Joshua 1:5–6 assures us of our Lord's perfect love for his children and of his eagerness to equip and empower his chosen servants. As magnificent as Moses was, Joshua was also called upon to do great things in settling the children of Israel in the land of Canaan. Whom the Lord calls, he qualifies.

APRIL 8

Have I not commanded thee? Be strong and of a good courage; be not afraid, neither be thou dismayed: for the Lord thy God is with thee whithersoever thou goest.

JOSHUA 1:9

At all times and in all dispensations, it takes courage and strength to exercise faith in the Lord. Living the gospel is not for the faint-hearted. President Thomas S. Monson wisely said: "Of course, we will face fear, experience ridicule, and meet opposition. Let us have the courage to defy the consensus, the courage to stand for principle. Courage, not compromise, brings the smile of God's approval. Courage becomes a living and an attractive virtue when it is regarded not only as a willingness to die manfully, but also as a determination to live decently. A moral coward is one who is afraid to do what he thinks is right because others will disapprove or laugh. Remember that all men have their fears, but those who face their fears with dignity have courage as well" (*Ensign,* May 2004, 55–56). The Lord will sustain us as we keep our covenants and go forward with faith.

APRIL 9

If ye do in any wise go back, and cleave unto the remnant of these nations . . . know for a certainty that . . . they shall be snares and traps unto you . . . , until ye perish from off this good land which the Lord your God hath given you.

JOSHUA 23:12–13

It is no easy thing to live among a people, befriend them, socialize with them, and yet draw a careful line between those we know and those we marry. Anciently, the Israelites were forbidden to socialize with the people of the land, but Latter-day-Saints in our day are charged to live in the world and make a difference for good. We cannot accomplish that charge without becoming friends and associates with those in the world. When it comes to marriage, however, we draw a careful line: we seek to be equally yoked in faith and lifestyle to those we marry.

APRIL 10

Choose you this day whom ye will serve . . .
but as for me and my house, we will serve the Lord.
JOSHUA 24:15

We cannot truly choose the Lord and the everlasting banquet his kingdom offers if we glance back longingly at Babylon, wondering what we're missing out on or secretly yearning for its perceived delights. "No man can serve two masters: for either he will hate the one, and love the other; or else he will hold to the one, and despise the other. Ye cannot serve God and mammon" (Matthew 6:24). Those with divided loyalties are halfhearted, feebly wanting both worlds. But the true Saints of God are committed to holding back the world, offending the devil with their devotion to truth, and honoring sacred covenants with complete fidelity. We serve the Lord by living the gospel, by loving and forgiving, by serving and sacrificing for others. We cannot fully grasp the iron rod if one hand is flailing aimlessly at the world's enticements. We must hold onto the iron rod with both hands.

APRIL 11

Nevertheless the Lord raised up judges. . . . And yet they would not hearken unto their judges, but they went a whoring after other gods, and bowed themselves unto them: they turned quickly out of the way which their fathers walked in.

JUDGES 2:16–17

Because Israel "went a whoring after other gods," God raised up judges to lead the people out of their wickedness and back into the light. Generally, these judges were military leaders or inspiring heroes who sought to rally the people of God to the Lord. In other words, the bride (the house of Israel, the Church) was unfaithful to the Bridegroom (the Lord God of Israel). They knew his laws, but they refused to keep them. They knew his statutes, but they violated them. They no doubt understood what was required to be holy, but they chose instead to be profane. Thus the anger of the Lord was poured out upon them, and for a season they forfeited the consummate blessings that ought to be enjoyed by a chosen people.

APRIL 12

And Deborah, a prophetess, the wife of Lapidoth, she judged Israel at that time.

JUDGES 4:4

One of the great figures in the Old Testament is Deborah. A woman appointed to be a judge of Israel, a woman who was possessed of the spirit of prophecy and revelation, Deborah was a leader with great courage and faith, a ready reminder that our God is no respecter of persons. Spiritual gifts and heavenly endowments are available to all of his children who prepare themselves to receive them, and there is nothing in the doctrine and teachings of Christ to suggest that the Almighty prefers or favors his sons over his daughters. Spiritual maturity and spiritual power are not gender specific.

APRIL 13

And the Lord said unto Gideon, The people that are with thee are too many for me to give the Midianites into their hands, lest Israel vaunt themselves against me, saying, Mine own hand hath saved me.

JUDGES 7:2

While our Heavenly Father desires that his children feel good about themselves as individuals, he is even more concerned that their confidence and total trust be centered in him. Humility is a difficult lesson to teach and an even more difficult quality to develop. It consists of recognizing our own weaknesses and limitations, recognizing how terribly reliant we are on divine assistance in conquering the Goliaths of our life and finding peace in the midst of unrest. In Judges, God purposely commands Gideon to reduce the size of his army to the point where it would have seemed embarrassingly difficult to face the Midianites, but only in this way could the victory that was forthcoming be recognized for what it was—a miraculous intervention of the heavenly hosts rallying in support of Israel. As the scriptures attest, God's power is made manifest in our lives when we acknowledge our own weakness before him (2 Corinthians 12:9–10; Ether 12:27).

APRIL 14

And the woman bare a son, and called his name Samson: and the child grew, and the Lord blessed him. And the Spirit of the Lord began to move him at times in the camp of Dan between Zorah and Eshtaol.

JUDGES 13:24–25

One of the most beloved and exciting stories of the Old Testament is that of Samson, the son of Manoah, a man of the tribe of Dan who was endowed by God with supernatural strength. Samson, born of a noble lineage, was set apart from the beginning as a child of promise, one who was placed under a Nazarite vow and dedicated wholly to the service of the Lord. Contrary to popular opinion, Samson's strength did not lie in the length of his hair but rather in the faithfulness of his life. Allowing the Philistine woman Delilah to cut his hair was but symbolic of Samson's allowing himself to be drawn into immorality and debauchery. Although Samson did much good for his people, his lack of consecration prevented him from accomplishing all that Jehovah would have had him do. The story of Samson is a story of tragedy, a story of what might have been.

APRIL 15

And Ruth said, Intreat me not to leave thee, or to return from following after thee: for whither thou goest, I will go; and where thou lodgest, I will lodge: thy people shall be my people, and thy God my God.

RUTH 1:16

Naomi and her two daughters-in-law, Orpah and Ruth, had all just lost their husbands to death. The words recorded in Ruth 1:16, one of the sweetest and most tender of all scriptural expressions, give us an insight into the soul of Ruth: she feels a deep love and loyalty to her mother-in-law and an attraction toward the religion of Jehovah. We suppose that she accepted the gospel and became a part of the community of believers. This story is important also because it demonstrates that God loves all of his children. How so? Ruth, a Moabitess, eventually marries Boaz, and their great-grandson becomes the man who unites the kingdom of Israel and is known as the mighty progenitor of the Messiah. In short, from Ruth comes David and eventually Jesus the Christ (Ruth 4:17; Matthew 1:5–6, 16).

APRIL 16

And the child Samuel ministered unto the Lord before Eli. And the word of the Lord was precious in those days; there was no open vision. That the Lord called Samuel: and he answered, Here am I.

1 SAMUEL 3:1, 4

The long prayed-for child Samuel was dedicated to the Lord by his mother, Hannah, and sent to live and work with the priest Eli. It appears that this was a time of great spiritual darkness in Israel, a season when vision and inspiration were scarce. God therefore began to teach the child Samuel to recognize his voice, to grow into the spirit of revelation. "Now Samuel did not yet know the Lord, neither was the word of the Lord yet revealed unto him" (1 Samuel 3:7). After responding three times to a voice that Samuel supposed was Eli's, the aged priest instructed Samuel that the voice was that of Jehovah and that he should pay heed to it. This simple story is mighty in the lesson it teaches: God calls upon each of us by his own voice—through our conscience, thoughts placed in our mind, and inspired feelings—line upon line, precept upon precept, until we become conversant with the language of the Lord.

APRIL 17

And the Lord said unto Samuel, Hearken unto the voice of the people in all that they say unto thee: for they have not rejected thee, but they have rejected me, that I should not reign over them.

1 SAMUEL 8:7

The Israelites came to Samuel the prophet and demanded that he provide for them a king "like all the nations" (1 Samuel 8:5). Samuel did his best to discourage the appointment of a king, knowing full well the atrocities and tragedies that follow in the wake of absolute power corrupting absolutely. Jehovah gave the same cautions and specific warnings about what happens to a people when an unrighteous monarch abuses his power and thereby corrupts society. Israel rejected these warnings and continued their pleadings. God therefore gave to the people what they wanted: a king. President Ezra Taft Benson said, "Sometimes He temporarily grants to men their unwise requests in order that they might learn from their own sad experiences. Some refer to this as the 'Samuel principle'" (*Teachings of Ezra Taft Benson,* 84).

APRIL 18

Beforetime in Israel, when a man went to enquire of God, thus he spake, Come, and let us go to the seer: for he that is now called a Prophet was beforetime called a Seer.

1 SAMUEL 9:9

Anciently, prophets were called seers. Although the roles of prophet and seer are obviously linked, Limhi and Ammon in the Book of Mormon teach us that a seer is greater than a prophet, for a seer is a prophet and a revelator also (Mosiah 8:16). Truly, "a seer can know of things which are past, and also of things which are to come, and by them shall all things be revealed, or . . . things which are not known shall be made known by them" (Mosiah 8:17). What a privilege is ours to live at a time when the gospel is on the earth in its fulness; when prophets, seers, and revelators walk the earth; when they seek for and obtain the mind and will of the Lord; when they see "things which [are] not visible to the natural eye" (Moses 6:36). Following them is our safety.

APRIL 19

The Spirit of the Lord will come upon thee, and thou shalt prophesy with them, and shalt be turned into another man. . . . And it was so, that when he had turned his back to go from Samuel, God gave him another heart.

1 Samuel 10:6–9

Those who are called to serve in the kingdom of God are charged to seek for the spirit of their calling, to obtain their errand from the Lord (Jacob 1:17). Each of us brings some dimension of our own strength and personality and capacity to an assignment, and this is as it should be. Breadth and diversity of backgrounds lead to freshness and spontaneity in the work of the Lord. And yet, it is vital that those who have been called to the ministry undergo the spiritual transformation that comes by the power of the Holy Spirit—the transformation that indeed turns us into another man or woman and gives to us another heart. As new creatures in Christ (2 Corinthians 5:17; Mosiah 27:26), we begin to acquire "the mind of Christ" (1 Corinthians 2:16) and therefore function in our calling as the Lord himself would do if he were laboring on earth.

APRIL 20

Only fear the Lord, and serve him in truth with all your heart: for consider how great things he hath done for you.

I SAMUEL 12:24

We fear the Lord because of our reverence and respect for his omnipotence, his goodness and mercy, and his loving kindness towards us, his children. We do not fear him as some authoritarian dictator or as some vengeful and ruthless tyrant. If he were such a tyrant, we would not seek him and serve him with all our hearts. If he were thus, we would be so blinded by trepidation that we could not contemplate his compassion and long-suffering toward his children. The fear that is reverence and respect is born of deep gratitude and abiding love. We know that without the Lord we have nothing. Without him we are nothing. Everything we have and are comes from God—our lives, our families, our opportunities and blessings, as well as our growing experiences and customized challenges. We show our thankfulness for the Lord by humbly serving him with love and commitment.

APRIL 21

Hath the Lord as great delight in burnt offerings and sacrifices, as in obeying the voice of the Lord? Behold, to obey is better than sacrifice, and to hearken than the fat of rams.

1 SAMUEL 15:22

While the law of sacrifice is at the heart of the gospel of Jesus Christ—indeed, the sacrifice of the Savior is the only reason we have a gospel or a plan of salvation by which fallen and mortal beings can be reconciled to exalted, immortal Deity—yet the Almighty expects his disciples to be diligent in their discipleship, to exercise that discipline and to gain that disposition that motivate them to keep the commandments and walk in the light. Our obedience must be linked with our sacrifice if we are to enjoy the fruits of our faith and if we are to please the God who has marked the path and led the way back to life eternal.

APRIL 22

Look not on his countenance, or on the height of his stature . . . for the Lord seeth not as man seeth; for man looketh on the outward appearance, but the Lord looketh on the heart.

1 SAMUEL 16:7

The Lord chose David to lead Israel not because of his stature or intellect but because of his heart. Likewise, in this last dispensation, the Lord chose Joseph Smith to usher in the fulness of times not because of his power or prestige but because of his heart. The Lord does the same with us: He sees us not as the world sees us because he looks on the heart. He who knows everything is not deceived by externals. He who fully discerns our heart is not fooled by appearances or glibness. He knows our past and present as well as our future, because he knows our heart. Isn't it reassuring to know that our perfect God, our all-knowing and all-loving Father, looks upon our heart—our desires, our intents, our willingness. No one else could stand in judgment; no one else could be our mediator or advocate but our merciful Lord (D&C 29:5).

APRIL 23

Then Samuel took the horn of oil, and anointed [David] in the midst of his brethren: and the Spirit of the Lord came upon David from that day forward.

1 SAMUEL 16:13

It has wisely been stated that whom the Lord calls, he qualifies. Individuals called to serve in the kingdom of God are not expected to do the job alone, to lift the heavy burdens or carry the weight without assistance. Nor should they attempt to do so. We will always have leaders, advisers, scriptures, and handbooks to counsel us and point the way. Most important, because this is the work of the Lord and he wants it done his way (D&C 64:29), we have the right to inspiration, to divine guidance, to the promptings and sweet whisperings of the Holy Ghost. It is by means of that Spirit that we find comfort when we feel overwhelmed, assurance and vitality when the course we have chosen is approved of God, and peace and joy when we serve diligently and with an eye single to the glory of God.

APRIL 24

Thou comest to me with a sword, and with a spear, and with a shield: but I come to thee in the name of the Lord of hosts.

1 SAMUEL 17:45

The forces of evil arrayed against us are awesome in their effects and impressive in their subtlety. Indeed, one of our severest challenges is the insidious influence of evil in its attractive and alluring enticements. Each day we face the giants of temptation and go to battle against the persuasive power of immorality and wickedness. It has ever been so. Three thousand years ago young David slew mighty Goliath with a sling and a stone and faith in the Lord. Today we resist the giants dedicated to our destruction by turning to the Lord with full purpose of heart. As Paul counseled, we "put on the whole armour of God, that [we] may be able to stand against the wiles of the devil" (Ephesians 6:11). The Lord will strengthen us in our desire to turn from evil and seek that which is "virtuous, lovely, or of good report or praiseworthy" (Articles of Faith 1:13). Girt about with the armor of God, we stand firm in righteousness.

APRIL 25

Therefore now let your hands be strengthened, and be ye valiant.

2 Samuel 2:7

The marvelous work and wonder of the Restoration requires sacrifice, courage, faith, and devotion. It rolls forth on the efforts of countless men and women, boys and girls, who are willing to do their part to stand for truth and strive for righteousness. It is not a work for spiritual cowards or for the weak-kneed fearful who remain on the fence, uncommitted to what the gospel requires or ashamed of its demands as they watch from the sidelines. We must be bold, yet humble; strong, yet meek; valiant, yet patient and long-suffering. As the apostle Paul said, "I am not ashamed of the gospel of Christ: for it is the power of God unto salvation to every one that believeth" (Romans 1:16). The Lord will surely strengthen us in our desire to be an "example of the believers, in word, in conversation, in charity, in spirit, in faith, in purity" (1 Timothy 4:12).

APRIL 26

Uzzah put forth his hand to the ark of God, and took hold of it; for the oxen shook it. And the anger of the Lord was kindled against Uzzah; and God smote him there for his error; and there he died by the ark of God.

2 Samuel 6:6–7

Uzzah's sudden death as a result of his effort to steady the ark has troubled Bible readers for centuries. We need first to recognize that we do not have a complete account of the story. Second, the seemingly stern God who ushered Uzzah into the next world is the same God who came to earth as Jesus of Nazareth, the Good Shepherd, the Prince of Peace. Third, Israel had to learn to comply implicitly with the Lord's statutes regarding the implements of the temple, which were important enough that he would take the life of a man for interfering with them. Fourth, although we view death with horror and finality, to God it is only a change in assignment, a transfer to another field of labor. To steady the ark—to step forward to assume a sacred role to which we have not been called—is thus unwise and ill advised. We must attend carefully to our own small plot of ground.

APRIL 27

And thine house and thy kingdom shall be established for ever before thee: thy throne shall be established for ever.

2 SAMUEL 7:16

While David, as a man of war, was not allowed to build the temple (that assignment would go to his son Solomon), he was promised that the kingdom of David would be established forever. Through David's lineage would come the One who would also be called David, the Second David, the Millennial David, even Jesus the Christ, the King of kings. Truly, "the government [would] be upon his shoulder. . . . Of the increase of his government and peace there shall be no end, upon the throne of David, and upon his kingdom, to order it, and to establish it with judgment and with justice from henceforth even for ever" (Isaiah 9:6–7).

David sent and enquired after the woman. And one said, Is not this Bath-sheba, the daughter of Eliam, the wife of Uriah the Hittite? And David sent messengers, and took her; and she came in unto him, and he lay with her.

2 SAMUEL 11:3–4

Surely there is no more heart-rending tragedy in the Old Testament than the fall of King David, the man after the Lord's own heart. In a critical moment David allowed his thoughts and feelings to run rampant and his affections to go unbridled: He committed adultery with Bathsheba, wife of Uriah. As serious as this sin was, David complicated it by arranging for Uriah to be killed in battle. His wanton immorality was thereby exacerbated by murder, the unforgivable sin. David thereby lost the Spirit of God as well as his exaltation hereafter (D&C 132:39). Although he was promised that his soul would not be left in hell (Psalm 16:10; Smith, *Teachings,* 339)—that he would be resurrected to a kingdom of glory—his psalms bespeak a broken man who never recovered what he had once been. Truly, vigilance is the price of victory in this life, for none of us is immune from sin.

APRIL 29

Then Amnon hated her exceedingly; so that the hatred wherewith he hated her was greater than the love wherewith he had loved her. And Amnon said unto her, Arise, be gone.

2 SAMUEL 13:15

Amnon, a vile and conniving son of David, plotted the sexual conquest of his beautiful stepsister Tamar. Recoiling from his demands, Tamar pleaded with him to go to their father, David, and request her hand in marriage. But Amnon was intent on other things, much more sordid—yielding to his lusts and stealing the virtue of an innocent one. We are taught the timeless and haunting lesson in 2 Samuel 13:15 that sexual involvement without the commitment and covenant associated with genuine love estranges. It breeds bitterness and hatred rather than genuine affection. Alma thus counseled his son Shiblon to "bridle all your passions, that ye may be filled with love" (Alma 38:12).

APRIL 30

The Lord is my rock, and my fortress, and my deliverer; the God of my rock; in him will I trust.

2 SAMUEL 22:2–3

King David repeatedly praised the Lord as his rock, his fortress, his deliverer, his source of strength and place of trust. He used other words as well: "He is my shield, and the horn of my salvation, my high tower, and my refuge, my saviour; thou savest me from violence" (2 Samuel 22:3). *Shield*—the Lord protects us as we battle the forces of evil; he is our shield and protection against the fiery darts of the adversary. *Horn of my salvation*—the Lord is the fount of saving grace through his infinite atonement. *High tower*—if we faithfully follow the word of the Lord, we will be lifted in our travails and exalted on high. *Refuge*—the Lord is our shelter from the storms of life, our safe haven amidst trials. *Saviour*—the Lord is the author of our salvation, "for there is none other name under heaven given among men, whereby we must be saved" (Acts 4:12).

May

Hear, O Israel:
The Lord our God is one Lord.
DEUTERONOMY 6:4

MAY 1

I go the way of all the earth: be thou strong therefore, and shew thyself a man; and keep the charge of the Lord thy God, to walk in his ways.

1 KINGS 2:2–3

Knowing his mortal days were coming to an end, King David exhorted his son Solomon to be strong and faithful in following the Lord. That is appropriate counsel for us all. Indeed, life presents opportunities, sorrows, and challenges that stretch our souls and educate our hearts. "All of us experience those wrenching, defining, difficult decisions that move us to a higher level of spirituality," said President James E. Faust. "They are the Gethsemanes of our lives that bring with them great pain and anguish. Sometimes they are too sacred to be shared publicly. They are the watershed experiences that help purge us of our unrighteous desires for the things of the world. As the scales of worldliness are taken from our eyes, we see more clearly who we are and what our responsibilities are concerning our divine destiny" (*Ensign,* November 2000, 59). As children of God, we must be strong in our determination to walk in the ways of the Lord.

MAY 2

And God gave Solomon wisdom and understanding exceeding much, and largeness of heart, even as the sand that is on the sea shore.

1 KINGS 4:29

The wisdom of Solomon exceeded that of all others of his time. He "spake three thousand proverbs: and his songs were a thousand and five" about relationships among nature, man, and God (1 Kings 4:32). His reign of forty years became legendary as a golden age of peace and prosperity in Israel's history (3 Nephi 13:29). The Lord granted him an understanding heart, riches and honor (1 Kings 3:12–13), and the privilege of building the temple in Jerusalem (1 Kings 5:5). Solomon was warned that if he abandoned the Lord's commandments to serve other gods, his kingdom would be cut off (1 Kings 9:1–9). Vital lessons about faithfulness and humility are to be found in Solomon's life. The greatest wisdom is in how we live our daily lives, for it is less what we *know* and more what we *do* that spells the difference between the natural man and the man of Christ. Truly, where much is given, much is required.

MAY 3

If thou wilt walk before me . . . in integrity of heart, and in uprightness, to do according to all that I have commanded thee, and . . . keep my statutes and my judgments: then I will establish the throne of thy kingdom upon Israel for ever.

1 KINGS 9:4–5

When the Lord appeared to Solomon for the second time, He promised great blessings if Israel was obedient and great cursings if they forsook Him (1 Kings 9:1–9). That promise remains in force. To the faithful come the blessings of "peace in this world, and eternal life in the world to come" (D&C 59:23). The wicked have no such promise. To the Lord's true followers, despite the challenges and heartaches of life, comes joy unspeakable both here and hereafter. The unrighteous have no such joy. To the charitable and honest in heart comes quiet confidence in the presence of the Lord (D&C 121:45). That divine endowment will be denied the ungodly. All blessings are predicated on our being peaceable disciples of the Lord who are true to the truth (D&C 130:20–21; 132:5). In the end, it is really very simple—Israel, ancient and modern, will be blessed as they walk the pathway of life with integrity and righteousness.

MAY 4

But king Solomon loved many strange women. For it came to pass, when Solomon was old, that his wives turned away his heart after other gods: and his heart was not perfect with the Lord his God, as was the heart of David his father.

1 KINGS 11:1, 4

In the Book of Mormon, Jacob condemns the unauthorized practice of plural marriage: "This people begin to wax in iniquity; they understand not the scriptures, for they seek to excuse themselves in committing whoredoms, because of the things which were written concerning David, and Solomon his son" (Jacob 2:23). David was guilty of adultery and murder. Solomon also took unauthorized wives who turned his heart away from the worship of Jehovah. Nathan and other prophets who held the sealing powers and the right to authorize plural marriages did not authorize such marriages (D&C 132:38–39). Thus the participants violated the law of God, opening themselves to spiritual death and their posterity to unspeakable tragedy.

Fear not; go and do as thou hast said: but make me thereof a little cake first, and bring it unto me, and after make for thee and for thy son. For thus saith the Lord God of Israel, The barrel of meal shall not waste, neither shall the cruse of oil fail.

1 KINGS 17:13–14

At first glance it seems odd, even selfish, that Elijah should ask the poor widow of Zarephath for anything at all, much less her last morsel of food. There she was, taking two sticks to prepare the fire to bake the last bit of meal and oil as a final dinner for herself and her son. Death in that day of bitter famine was lurking near at hand. And then Elijah instructed her to make him a cake first! Her kindness, her obedience, and her sacrifice—these were rewarded by the prophetic promise that not only would she and her child survive the famine but would never go without again. As we sing in the hymn, "Sacrifice brings forth the blessings of heaven" (*Hymns,* no. 27). Like another widow described in the New Testament (Mark 12:41–44), the widow of Zarephath gave all that she had, and her simple consecration did not go unnoticed by the God of nature.

MAY 6

And Elijah came unto all the people, and said, How long halt ye between two opinions? if the Lord be God, follow him: but if Baal, then follow him. And the people answered him not a word.

1 KINGS 18:21

Life is a series of choices. President James E. Faust said, "In this life we have to make many choices. [They] determine to a large extent our happiness or our unhappiness, because we have to live with the consequences of our choices. Making perfect choices all of the time is not possible. It just doesn't happen. But it is possible to make good choices we can live with and grow from" (*Ensign,* May 2004, 51). When we make a choice, we choose a consequence. If we choose sin and sloth, we eventually reap the consequences of unhappiness and despair. If we choose to live on the edge of righteousness, with one foot in Zion and the other in Babylon, we reap in due course the consequences of misery and fear. But those who live firmly on the Lord's side of the line reap the consequences of peace and solace, love and contentment, the joy of redemption and the hope of eternal life.

A great and strong wind rent the mountains . . . ;
but the Lord was not in the wind: . . . but the Lord was not in the earthquake: . . . but the Lord was not in the fire: and after the fire a still small voice.

1 KINGS 19:11–12

Revelation whispers to our hearts in the still small voice of the Spirit. As children of God, if we humbly seek the Lord and diligently strive to serve him with full purpose of heart, we will have the spirit of comfort and guidance poured out upon us as the dews of heaven. President Gordon B. Hinckley said, "There has come to you as your birthright something beautiful and sacred and divine. Never forget that. Your Eternal Father is the great Master of the universe. He rules over all, but He also will listen to your prayers . . . and hear you as you speak with Him. He will answer your prayers. He will not leave you alone" (*Ensign,* May 2004, 112). We are never alone when we have the light of the Lord to guide and succor us.

MAY 8

And after the earthquake a fire; but the Lord was not in the fire: and after the fire a still small voice.

1 KINGS 19:12

The voice of the Lord distills softly upon the mind and heart. It does not shout or scream, bellow or bark. It whispers quietly to those who humbly listen for the Lord's will. Elder Henry B. Eyring taught: "I have had prayers answered. Those answers were most clear when what I wanted was silenced by an overpowering need to know what God wanted. It is then that the answer from a loving Heavenly Father can be spoken to the mind by the still, small voice and can be written on the heart" (*Ensign,* November 2000, 86). To receive the Lord's will, we must separate ourselves from the noise of the world and strive to live righteously, obeying the commandments and loving and serving our fellow beings. To listen for the Lord's promptings, we must take time for holiness—time for solitude and stillness, for pondering and quiet contemplation. The voice of the Lord gently beckons as it inspires us to seek the things of eternity.

MAY 9

And he took the mantle of Elijah that fell from him, and smote the waters, and said, Where is the Lord God of Elijah? and when he also had smitten the waters, they parted hither and thither: and Elisha went over.

2 KINGS 2:14

Elisha had watched his mentor and prophetic leader Elijah perform miracle after miracle. He had witnessed as Elijah drew upon the power of the priesthood to accomplish what most would have considered impossible. Having now received the responsibility and the prophetic mantle descend upon him (in this case an actual cloak or robe, but in general a heavenly endowment of power), Elisha set about the task of ministering to the people in much the same way that his master had, even raising the dead. "Where is the Lord God of Elijah?" is another way of proclaiming, "I have been called to succeed a mighty prophet, to act in the name of the God of Abraham, Isaac, and Jacob. To do so, I must enjoy a like endowment to that which was enjoyed by Elijah. Where is that power? May it now be poured out upon me!" And so it was.

MAY 10

And Elisha sent a messenger unto him, saying, Go and wash in Jordan seven times, and thy flesh shall come again to thee, and thou shalt be clean.

2 KINGS 5:10

Thousands of years ago leprosy-afflicted Naaman learned a guiding truth: When the prophet speaks, it is wise to follow. What the Lord's spokesman says may not make perfect sense or it may seem simple or strange, but when the prophet speaks, it is the Lord himself speaking (D&C 1:38). Would we be more inclined to follow if the prophet asked of us some great thing? Many are willing to leave home to serve the Lord in high-profile assignments in faraway places; fewer are willing to serve in low-recognition callings. Some are prepared to relocate to Jackson County; fewer are anxious to attend the temple regularly and read scriptures daily. The Lord needs faithful Primary teachers, dedicated home and visiting teachers, devoted Saints who humbly, faithfully serve others and build the kingdom. The Lord and his prophets usually do not ask us to do dramatic and unusual things. But blessings will be poured out upon us as we follow their counsel (D&C 21:4–6).

Lord, I pray thee, open his eyes, that he may see. And the Lord opened the eyes of the young man; and he saw: and, behold, the mountain was full of horses and chariots of fire.
2 KINGS 6:17

Thank heaven we are not left alone in this life, without aid in our trials or strength to resist temptation. "In the gospel of Jesus Christ you have help from both sides of the veil and you must never forget that," counseled Jeffrey R. Holland. "When disappointment and discouragement strike—and they will—you remember and never forget that if our eyes could be opened we would see horses and chariots of fire as far as the eye can see riding at reckless speed to come to our protection (2 Kgs. 6:16–17). They will always be there, these armies of heaven, in defense of Abraham's seed" (*New Era,* October 1980, 15). We must open our eyes and hearts to the bountiful blessings around us: good people who teach and help us, scriptures and inspired leaders who fortify us, God's creations and the power of prayer that lift our spirits, and so much more. Always remember that there are those on both sides of the veil who will rally round us.

MAY 12

In the ninth year of Hoshea the king of Assyria took Samaria, and carried Israel away into Assyria, and placed them in Halah and in Habor by the river of Gozan, and in the cities of the Medes.

2 KINGS 17:6

Having strayed from the religion of Jehovah (the gospel of Jesus Christ), the ten northern tribes were "scattered to and fro" and "lost" to the knowledge of the rest of the world (1 Nephi 22:4). Myths and legends abound as to their whereabouts and their return, but both ancient and modern revelation attest that they are scattered among the nations and will be gathered as everyone else is gathered—through conversion to the gospel. That is, in our day and in the future they will respond to the message of salvation as delivered by the Latter-day Saints, will be baptized, confirmed, endowed, and sealed as families in holy places. While we have in a sense been gathering the lost tribes since 1830—inasmuch as Joseph is one of the northern tribes—the risen Lord declared plainly that the great day of their gathering lies ahead: It is millennial (3 Nephi 21:25–26).

MAY 13

And the covenant that I have made with you ye shall not forget; neither shall ye fear other gods. But the Lord your God ye shall fear; and he shall deliver you out of the hand of all your enemies.

2 KINGS 17:38–39

Faithfulness always casts out fear. The Lord's promise is sure: "I, the Lord, am bound when ye do what I say; but when ye do not what I say, ye have no promise" (D&C 82:10). When we enter into covenant with the Savior and humbly strive to follow and serve him with full purpose of heart, we need not fear. Although we will not be immune to sorrow and heartache or the trials and vicissitudes of life, we will be delivered from enduring fear by exercising faith in the Lord. We are delivered from fear every time we obey the principles of the gospel and go forward with confidence in the Lord. We are delivered from fear as we turn to heaven in sincere prayer and in quiet, Spirit-filled pondering of the great plan of happiness. The Lord is always on the side of the righteous. And the righteous are those who daily are doing their best to live the gospel, love their fellowman, and serve the Lord.

MAY 14

Reuben [was] the firstborn of Israel . . . ; but, forasmuch as he defiled his father's bed, his birthright was given unto the sons of Joseph the son of Israel. . . . Judah prevailed above his brethren, and of him came the chief ruler; but the birthright was Joseph's.

1 CHRONICLES 5:1–2

Reuben, the firstborn of Jacob, was heir to the birthright but lost that privilege when he committed serious sin. Instead of the birthright then passing to Simeon, the secondborn son of Leah, it passed to Joseph, the firstborn of Rachel. That birthright entitled Joseph to a double portion of Jacob's inheritance, but more important, it gave him the right to the keys (the right of presidency or directing power) of the Melchizedek Priesthood. In that ancient day, priesthood leaders presided over a patriarchal theocracy, a family government that received direction from on high. These mighty high priests governed in all things civil and ecclesiastical. Revelation was their constitution, and continuing inspiration was the basis for their laws.

MAY 15

For they cried to God in the battle, and he was intreated of them; because they put their trust in him.
1 CHRONICLES 5:20

In all dispensations, those who trust in God find succor and hope. Helaman recounted that his stripling warriors were strengthened in their battles "because of their exceeding faith in that which they had been taught to believe—that there was a just God, and whosoever did not doubt, that they should be preserved by his marvelous power. Now this was the faith of these of whom I have spoken; they are young, and their minds are firm, and they do put their trust in God continually" (Alma 57:26–27). No matter our age, no matter the time or place, those who put their trust in God are blessed. They'll still face the battles of life that are common to all: disappointment, disease, worry, heartache— but their faith helps them to see with the long-range, wide-angle lens of eternity. They'll continually face the conflicts of good and evil, virtue and vice, but come out victorious because of their firm faith in the Lord Jesus Christ.

MAY 16

Give thanks unto the Lord, call upon his name, make known his deeds among the people. Sing unto him, sing psalms unto him, talk ye of all his wondrous works.

1 CHRONICLES 16:8–9

Some three thousand years ago, David pitched his tent and offered burnt sacrifices and peace offerings before God. Afterward, David blessed the people in the name of the Lord and fed them. He then delivered his first psalm of thanksgiving (1 Chronicles 16:1–7). His words echo down the centuries: "O give thanks unto the Lord; for he is good; for his mercy endureth for ever" (1 Chronicles 16:34). Today and always, we acknowledge the Lord; we call upon his name in humility and thankfulness and bear witness to the world of his goodness and mercy. We sing praises unto him for his bounteous love and inexhaustible gospel. We offer our broken heart and contrite spirit as we come unto him and access the power of the infinite atonement (2 Nephi 2:7). We talk of his wondrous works and show our gratitude by the way we live our lives. In every moment, let us give thanks unto the Lord.

MAY 17

Glory ye in his holy name: let the heart of them rejoice that seek the Lord. Seek the Lord and his strength, seek his face continually.

1 CHRONICLES 16:10–11

Always with thanksgiving, we "remember [the Lord's] marvellous works that he hath done, his wonders, and the judgments of his mouth" (1 Chronicles 16:12). An attitude of gratitude is one of the key requisites for seeking after the Lord. If we seek the Lord with thankfulness, desire his righteousness with all our hearts, and come unto him in meekness and humility, we will find rest in him. "For every one that asketh receiveth; and he that seeketh findeth; and to him that knocketh it shall be opened" (Matthew 7:8). Seeking and rejoicing are one and the same. Sincere seekers, despite setbacks and shortcomings, always find eventual cause for rejoicing—here and hereafter. And those with hearts full of thankfulness will in time find the Lord whom they seek. As we seek him, we are strengthened by his perfect strength and comforted by his redeeming love.

MAY 18

Be of good courage, and let us behave ourselves valiantly for our people, and for the cities of our God: and let the Lord do that which is good in his sight.

1 CHRONICLES 19:13

Hundreds of years ago the Lord assisted Israel in defeating the Ammonites and the Syrians. Their battle cry was faithfulness to the Lord and courage in the face of a powerful enemy. We likewise face formidable foes today—adversaries that would lure us into paths of wickedness and destroy us in their evil designs. Our primary battles today are fought within the soul, in the quiet chambers of the heart. Will we shun evil and hold back the world? Does our thinking and behaving reflect Zion or Babylon? Are we valiant in our testimonies of truth? Do we do our best to follow the Lord and seek his righteousness? To stand strong against the wiles of the adversary, we must be humble and faithful, steadfast and immovable. In our hearts and in our homes, we strive to live in the best interests of present and future generations. Truly, we are in the Lord's hands. Our prayer and sole desire are that we do his will.

MAY 19

For the Lord searcheth all hearts, and understandeth all the imaginations of the thoughts: if thou seek him, he will be found of thee; but if thou forsake him, he will cast thee off for ever.

1 CHRONICLES 28:9

In ancient Israel David gathered to Jerusalem all the princes of Israel and the tribes, the captains of the companies, the stewards over all the possessions of the king, the leaders and officers, the mighty and valiant men (1 Chronicles 28:1). At this assembly David appointed his son Solomon to build the temple and sit upon the throne of the kingdom of Israel (1 Chronicles 28:5–6). With the wisdom of sorrow and regret, David exhorted his son, "And thou, Solomon my son, know thou the God of thy father, and serve him with a perfect heart and with a willing mind" (1 Chronicles 28:9). David's life illustrates the need for each of us to endure in faithfulness to the end. As a youth he was a man after the Lord's "own heart" (1 Samuel 13:14). But because of his sins, David is suffering a serious penalty for his disobedience to the commandments of God and has fallen from his exaltation (D&C 132:39).

Take heed now; for the Lord hath chosen thee to build an house for the sanctuary: be strong, and do it.
1 CHRONICLES 28:10

The words of David to his son Solomon, who was charged with building the temple, echo down the centuries of time: "Be strong, and do it." In the premortal realm we rose up in favor of the Father's plan—it took strength to vote for agency and the plan of happiness. Adam and Eve, our first parents, exercised great faith as they were driven out of the Garden of Eden, and both physical and spiritual death came into the world upon all mankind (Helaman 14:16–17). Today it certainly takes courage to build our foundation upon Christ and stand fast against the enticements of the world and the mighty winds of the adversary (Helaman 5:12). It takes sincere dedication to stay steadfast and immovable in keeping the commandments of the Lord (Mosiah 5:15). The Lord has chosen each one of us for a unique mission in life; truly, no one can take our place—we must be strong and do it.

MAY 21

Be strong and of good courage, and do it: fear not, nor be dismayed: for the Lord God, even my God, will be with thee.

1 CHRONICLES 28:20

Before he died, King David gave Solomon the pattern and materials for building the temple. David exhorted his son to faithfulness and courage, "for the Lord God, even my God, will be with thee; he will not fail thee, nor forsake thee, until thou hast finished all the work for the service of the house of the Lord" (1 Chronicles 28:20). When the Lord wants a temple built, he will provide the way and means. In our dispensation it is the same. From the time of Joseph Smith to our day when temples are beginning to dot the earth, the Lord inspires his prophet to build temples at the right time and in the right place. The financial condition of the faithful, be it poverty or abundance, the forces of evil arrayed against the building of the temple, or lack of knowledge and expertise, or any other possible hindrance or difficulty makes no difference—when the Lord wants a temple built, it will be built.

MAY 22

God appear[ed] unto Solomon, and said unto him, Ask what I shall give thee. And Solomon said unto God, . . . Give me now wisdom and knowledge.

2 CHRONICLES 1:7–10

When God offered Solomon any gift he desired, he could have asked for long life, power over his enemies, or vast riches. Instead, the king asked for an understanding heart to judge Israel, a compassionate heart that opens the door to wisdom (1 Kings 3:5–15). If God offered you the same gift, what would you ask for? Fame, fortune, happiness, health? The wisdom of Solomon's request teaches us much about life and living. Wisdom is a product of heartfelt concern for others. True joy comes from reaching out to others in love and empathy. After all, what can we ever really know of another's fears, frustrations, and disappointments? How can we become sensitive to others if we haven't looked into their hearts and sought for deeper understanding? In our own moments of sorrow, is anything needed more than the compassion that opens one heart to another? Indeed, the legendary wisdom of Solomon comes from an understanding heart.

MAY 23

Believe in the Lord your God, so shall ye be established; believe his prophets, so shall ye prosper.

2 CHRONICLES 20:20

King Jehoshaphat's faithful admonition to the people of Judah and their dutiful response saved them from their enemies. The faith of the king and the people, coupled with their thanks and praise to the Lord, enabled them to vanquish their foes and return to Jerusalem in peace. Then, as now, the key is to believe the Lord and have faith in his purposes, to believe his anointed prophets and know they are called of the Lord, and to remain true to the principles of everlasting truth. If we believe in the Lord, we will believe in his prophets. And if we follow the Lord's earthly leaders, we will reap the promised harvest of the abundant life and enjoy the greatest gift of God, which is eternal life (D&C 14:7). Several times during the year in conferences of the Church, we have opportunity to raise our arm in signifying our sustaining vote for the leaders the Lord has called. May we do so with humility and gratitude.

MAY 24

Thus saith God, Why transgress ye the commandments of the Lord, that ye cannot prosper? because ye have forsaken the Lord, he hath also forsaken you.

2 CHRONICLES 24:20

A father and mother and their four children have a family motto: "If you want to be happy, be good." Two thousand years ago, Alma said it to his son this way: "Wickedness never was happiness" (Alma 41:10). There is no enduring peace, no lasting joy, for those who forsake the Lord and his proven pathway to happiness. The Lord said, "I will not succor my people in the day of their transgression; but I will hedge up their ways that they prosper not. . . . If my people shall sow filthiness they shall reap the chaff thereof in the whirlwind; and the effect thereof is poison" (Mosiah 7:29–30). We turn away from the Lord through the poison of sin, through the venom of pride and apathy and laziness. The promise is sure: we will prosper if we "turn to the Lord with full purpose of heart, and put [our] trust in him, and serve him with all diligence of mind" (Mosiah 7:33).

MAY 25

And he did that which was right in the sight of the Lord, but not with a perfect heart.
2 CHRONICLES 25:2

Sometimes we do the right things for the wrong reasons. We obey because it's convenient or others might be watching or we expect a reward. We obey out of fear or a desire for self-aggrandizement or because it's the way we've always done it. But the Lord wants our whole hearts, our entire being. He wants us to exemplify integrity in our lives, to embody inside-out congruence in daily living, to walk the talk. Heartfelt devotion comes from deep conversion to gospel truth and is demonstrated over the course of a lifetime. Our wholehearted obedience must flow from the love we have for the Lord and from our respect for his commandments. The Savior said, "He that hath my commandments, and keepeth them, he it is that loveth me: and he that loveth me shall be loved of my Father, and I will love him" (John 14:21). As we hold nothing back and love the Lord with our whole hearts, we will do that which is right in his sight.

MAY 26

For the Lord your God is gracious and merciful,
and will not turn away his face from you, if ye return unto him.
2 CHRONICLES 30:9

God's love for us is constant and will not diminish, his arm is forever stretched out to his children, but he cannot rescue us from painful consequences of wrong choices. He is a God of justice and chastisement, but he is also a God of perfect mercy and grace, a caring Redeemer who saves us from sin, suffering, and death through his infinite atonement. The Lord does not hold grudges or withhold love, compassion, and forgiveness for those who are meek and repentant. He has promised: "Draw near unto me and I will draw near unto you; seek me diligently and ye shall find me; ask, and ye shall receive; knock, and it shall be opened unto you" (D&C 88:63). He alone can be our judge, because only he knows what shaped who we are, what our deepest desires and real intents have been, what our charity amounted to, and how we have drawn upon the power of the Atonement.

MAY 27

For there be more with us than with him: With him is an arm of flesh; but with us is the Lord our God to help us, and to fight our battles.

2 CHRONICLES 32:7–8

As we face the challenges of life, we must remember the biblical words: "Be strong and courageous, be not afraid nor dismayed for the king of Assyria, nor for all the multitude that is with him" (2 Chronicles 32:7). The king of Assyria and the multitudes arrayed against us may be health problems, financial setbacks, injustice and persecution in its various forms. Also arrayed against us are the forces of evil in the world, which are escalating their efforts to destroy virtue in the land and faith in the Lord. But if we are soft-hearted, if we are steadfast and immovable in keeping our covenants, the Lord and all the faithful stand ready to sustain us. Righteousness is vastly more powerful, more pervasive and potent than the puny arm of flesh. When the Lord is with us, it matters not who is against us or what challenges we face.

In the first year of Cyrus king of Persia, that the word of the Lord by the mouth of Jeremiah might be fulfilled, the Lord stirred up the spirit of Cyrus king of Persia, that he made a proclamation throughout all his kingdom, and put it also in writing.

EZRA 1:1

God works through all his children, even those who have not embraced the covenant gospel, in order to accomplish his grand purposes. Cyrus, king of Persia, did that which was prophesied he would do: He opened the door for the children of Israel to return to their homeland and rebuild their temple. We do not know what kind of a man Cyrus was, but we know that he was in a position of great importance, a position through which Jehovah could work to deliver the children of Israel from captivity and their scattered condition. To be sure, revelation generally comes to those who have been baptized and confirmed members of the Church of Jesus Christ, but the God of heaven will make exceptions when it is needful.

And they sang together by . . . praising and giving thanks unto the Lord; because he is good. . . . And all the people shouted with a great shout . . . , because the foundation of the house of the Lord was laid.

EZRA 3:11

In every dispensation, the spirit of rejoicing and thanksgiving has accompanied temple building. From anticipation of its announcement to laying the foundation to completion and dedication, the Saints praise the name of the Lord for his goodness and mercy in giving them a house of the Lord. Hearts full of gratitude, on both sides of the veil, join together as a holy sanctuary is constructed, a place in which sacred ceremonies and ordinances are performed, a place where the Spirit of the Lord dwells, a place where the Lord may come. Today, as in times past, in solemn assemblies the Spirit of God burns like a fire as we sing and shout with the armies of heaven:

Hosanna to God and the Lamb!
Let glory to them in the highest be given,
Henceforth and forever,
Amen and amen! ("The Spirit of God like a Fire," Hymns, *no. 2*).

MAY 30

Then the people of the land weakened the hands of the people of Judah, and troubled them in building.

EZRA 4:4

The Israelites (specifically, members of the tribes of Judah and Benjamin) had begun the work of rebuilding the temple. The people of the land, those not of the faith, sought to distract them from their labors and harass them in their duties. Later, when the builders were invited to cease their work to have extended conversations with those on the ground, the leaders of the Israelites insisted that the work in which they were engaged was too sacred and too important to be interrupted by chit chat. How often in our own lives we are invited to put aside the weightier matters of life in order to spend time with our own distracters and thus with lesser things. Happiness and success in life come through focusing our energies on matters of eternal import and learning to say no when distractions arise. The deepest enjoyments of life, leading to the greatest joys hereafter, derive from staying at our duty station until our work is completed.

MAY 31

The people of Israel . . . have not separated themselves from the people of the lands, . . . for they have taken of their daughters for themselves, and for their sons: so that the holy seed have mingled themselves with the people of those lands.

EZRA 9:1–2

Marriage is so much more than a civil rite, so much more significant than a legal ceremony, so vastly superior to a social arrangement. Marriage was instituted by God in the Garden of Eden. He intended for the union between Adam and Eve to last forever. Marriage outside the covenant does not produce the same level and depth of commitment that marriage within the covenant provides, nor does it give the eternal perspective necessary when challenges, traumas, and tragedies in life arise. Marriage in the house of the Lord, bound for time and all eternity, is God's way of perpetuating the blessings of Abraham, Isaac, and Jacob. It is his way of bringing greater light into a darkened world.

June

Choose you this day whom ye will serve . . . : but as for me and my house, we will serve the Lord.

Joshua 24:15

JUNE 1

So built we the wall; and all the wall was joined together unto the half thereof: for the people had a mind to work.

NEHEMIAH 4:6

Nehemiah was a leader whose passion for Jerusalem drove him to leave the security of his life in Persia to oversee the rebuilding of a protective wall around the city. Although he faced many difficulties, the job was finished in record time. Leadership requires courage and determination. It demands vision and tenacity. It means we're willing to roll up our sleeves and get to work. Opportunities to prove our dedication occur most often in quiet, private places. Staying with something or someone over the long haul—maintaining the vision and keeping the commitment year after year—is the surest manifestation of a courageous heart. Taking on the daily tasks of life with hope and faith, with kindness and respect, is an indication of our desire to follow the Lord. May we influence others by setting an example of courage and hard work: "Let us not be weary in well doing: for in due season we shall reap, if we faint not" (Galatians 6:9).

JUNE 2

And Ezra the priest brought the law before the congregation both of men and women, and all that could hear with understanding. So they read in the book in the law of God distinctly, and gave the sense, and caused them to understand the reading.

NEHEMIAH 8:2, 8

For some seventy years the Israelites had been in captivity. During the Babylonian exile, Aramaic (a Semitic sister language of Hebrew) had become the common language of the people. It had been many years since the rank and file among the descendants of Jacob had heard the scriptures read aloud and rejoiced in the feelings and insights that flow from hearing the word of God. On this occasion, Ezra the priest offered reverence for the scripture by standing, reading from the Hebrew, and providing an Aramaic paraphrase (*targum*) to holy writ. Ezra's pattern for teaching became the pattern for reading and interpreting scripture for generations, one that was followed by the Savior himself when he stood up to read from Isaiah 61 (a messianic prophecy) in the synagogue in Nazareth (Luke 4:16–21).

JUNE 3

Stand up and bless the Lord your God for ever and ever. . . . thou hast made heaven, . . . the earth, and all things that are therein, the seas, and all that is therein, and thou preservest them all.

NEHEMIAH 9:5–6

We owe everything we have, our very lives and the air we breathe to the Lord, our Creator. He has formed and preserved this world for our benefit. His fount of love pours down from heaven in the beauties around us and in his blessings large and small. King Benjamin said, "If ye should serve him who has created you from the beginning, and is preserving you from day to day, by lending you breath, that ye may live and move and do according to your own will, and even supporting you from one moment to another—I say, if ye should serve him with all your whole souls yet ye would be unprofitable servants" (Mosiah 2:21). No matter what we do we still, and forever will, fall short. Remember the words of the apostle Paul: "For all have sinned, and come short of the glory of God; being justified freely by his grace through the redemption that is in Christ Jesus" (Romans 3:23–24). Praise the Lord's name forever.

JUNE 4

Thou art a God ready to pardon, gracious and merciful, slow to anger, and of great kindness.

NEHEMIAH 9:17

Believers in all dispensations have come to know the eternal truth that our Father in Heaven is a loving God who is gracious, merciful, and ready to forgive. He has given his Only Begotten Son as a sinless ransom for sin, the "propitiation for our sins" (1 John 2:2; 4:9–10; John 3:16). Jesus Christ offers us his infinite and intimate atonement to pay the price of our individual sins and to comfort us in our pain and heartache. Because, ultimately, forgiveness is a gift of God's grace that descends upon all who receive it, whatever forgiveness we extend to others is a reflection of the forgiveness God so generously showers upon us. Forgiveness heals as it cleanses the heart and mind of hate's poison. Anger and animosity keep wounds open; bitterness and resentment destroy. Just as God offers us his mercy and forgiveness, so we can extend our hand to those around us who ask for our pardon, who need our compassion and kindness.

JUNE 5

Who knoweth whether thou art
come to the kingdom for such a time as this?
ESTHER 4:14

Each of us comes to earth as a part of a divine plan. We can rest assured that none of us is here by accident or that when we were born and where we were born were simply matters of chance. There is a grand plan of salvation, a plan of God the Father, which was put into operation through the call and appointment and ordination of the Savior Jesus Christ. This great plan of happiness makes the blessings of the gospel of God available to every human soul, whether in this life or in the life to come. But each one of us has an individualized plan, and no doubt there are things we are sent here to do—people to influence, assignments to carry out, lessons to learn—that we and we alone can do best. The God and Father of us all is depending upon us to do what we were sent here to do. We must not fail.

JUNE 6

So will I go in unto the king, which is not according to the law: and if I perish, I perish.
ESTHER 4:16

With abiding faith and steadfast courage, Esther told Mordecai and the Jews to fast for three days and three nights prior to her going to see the king. Esther also fasted and drew upon the powers of heaven in behalf of her people. This was a time for spiritual preparation, for prayer and pondering at this crucial point in Jewish history. She placed her life in the hands of God and the king. We can almost hear her say, "Thy will be done." This was her moment of truth, and she was determined to see it through. Her fearless leadership and meek willingness to endanger her own life, if need be, to save her people is a model of committed discipleship. To go to the king unsummoned was a capital offense. Although her life was in jeopardy, a greater calling and divine charge sent her forward with faith. With humble resignation, knowing that God knows all things and she was on his errand, she went to the king.

JUNE 7

There was a man in the land of Uz, whose name was Job; and that man was perfect and upright, and one that feared God, and eschewed evil.

JOB 1:1

Job was "perfect and upright, . . . one that feared God, and eschewed evil" (Job 1:1). There is no question that Job was a man possessed of great righteousness, one who had given his heart and soul to Jehovah and covenanted to serve him at all hazards. But how was Job perfect? Was he completely without flaw? Did he never make a mistake or take a spiritual detour? No. Job was perfect in the sense that his life was whole, complete, and mature. Because he remained in covenant with the Lord, that Lord made him perfect (Moroni 10:32; D&C 76:69). On his own, Job was weak just as we are. With Christ, he was mighty and strong. Left to his own resources, Job was incomplete; with Christ, he was complete. In his daily walk and talk, Job was imperfect, but as he sought to walk with the Lord and to maintain "the mind of Christ" (1 Corinthians 2:16), he was perfect.

JUNE 8

And the Lord said unto Satan, Hast thou considered my servant Job, that there is none like him in the earth, a perfect and an upright man, one that feareth God, and escheweth evil?

JOB 1:8

Satan obtained leave from the Lord to tempt and try righteous Job, just as Satan may tempt and try every mortal soul. The narrative of Job is an example, a type and shadow, of the predicament of us all: To one degree or another, each of us may relate Job's experiences to the tests and trials of life. Ours may not be as severe, but they test us nonetheless. The trials of life can expand our hearts, deepen our commitment to everlasting things, strengthen faith and relationships, and steel our resolve to serve the Lord at all costs. They can also embitter and destroy us. How we respond to temptation proves our character. How we respond to disappointment and heartache manifests our faith and steadfastness. How we respond to trials and vicissitudes demonstrates our willingness to submit. Like Job's, our trials can be steppingstones to greater faithfulness and devotion or stumbling blocks that lead to despair.

JUNE 9

Happy is the man whom God correcteth:
therefore despise not thou the chastening of the Almighty.

JOB 5:17

The Lord chastens those whom he loves (D&C 95:1). God loves with a perfect love all his spirit sons and daughters. The Lord calls us to become new creatures in him, to be born anew and become alive in him, to endure chastening so that we can become sanctified heirs of eternal life (D&C 101:5). If we are too proud or preoccupied to bear chastisement, we are not worthy of the glory of Zion or of the kingdom of God (D&C 136:31). If we resent the counsel of inspired leaders and harden our hearts against them, we will not enjoy peace and joy here or hereafter. Pride slams the door to exaltation. This life is our time of probation and tutoring. We are here to repent and forgive, to learn and grow, to be taught by a loving God through his anointed leaders how we can progress along the pathway to celestial reward and everlasting happiness.

JUNE 10

My soul is weary of my life. Wherefore then hast thou brought me forth out of the womb?

JOB 10:1, 18

Who among us has not become discouraged and tired of the difficulties of life? The life of Job provides a model of faithfulness despite challenges and hope amidst despair. Like Job, perhaps we too ask why we are here, what the purpose of our life may be, and how we are supposed to continue in faith when surrounded by trials and temptations. But a reassuring voice from heaven touches our soul: We are here to love and serve the Lord and our neighbors; we are here to grow in righteousness and share our testimonies; we are here to overcome the world and become Saints "through the atonement of Christ the Lord, and [become] as a child, submissive, meek, humble, patient, full of love, willing to submit to all things which the Lord seeth fit to inflict upon [us], even as a child doth submit to his father" (Mosiah 3:19). This is the purpose of life.

JUNE 11

If I be wicked, woe unto me; and if I be righteous, yet will I not lift up my head. I am full of confusion; therefore see thou mine affliction.

JOB 10:15

Most of us, like Job of old, carry on a dialogue within ourselves. We lament our "natural man" susceptibilities and know that we are in need of repentance. We also know that sometimes we get things right, we overcome the flesh and put off the natural man—even so, we are in need of meekness. This is the "confusion" of mortality—we aren't perfect and we make mistakes; we take steps forward and then a step back; we learn and grow and then forget and stumble. To become spiritually strengthened we must go forward with faith in the Lord, with devotion to truth, with integrity and humility of heart. Even in our sinfulness we cannot give up hope. And in our righteous endeavors we cannot become proud and self-satisfied. We're never finished. Like Job and Nephi, we must endure in faithfulness to the end and put our trust in the Lord (2 Nephi 4:15–35).

JUNE 12

Though he slay me, yet will I trust in him:
but I will maintain mine own ways before him.

JOB 13:15

Those who have learned to surrender their all to God have also learned that whatever God chooses to do with their life—even taking it—is fine with them. Abraham's faith was manifest in his willingness to offer his covenant son, Isaac, in sacrifice, when Jehovah had promised to raise up a mighty posterity through Isaac. But Abraham obeyed even in the face of the seemingly absurd, "accounting that God was able to raise him up, even from the dead" (Hebrews 11:19). Similarly, Job's trust in God was implicit and empathic: he was ready to follow the divine will, no matter the cost. Truly, God's ways are not our ways; God's thoughts are not our thoughts (Isaiah 55:8–9). Let us not forget that he is omnipotent and omniscient. The wisest among us come to trust him, no matter what.

JUNE 13

For I know that my redeemer liveth, and that he shall stand at the latter day upon the earth: And though after my skin worms destroy this body, yet in my flesh shall I see God.

JOB 19:25–26

We all need reminders that there is life beyond this one. True life. Eternal life. Glorious life. In a sense we're all like Job as we sojourn through mortality, battling disease and discouragement, sorrow and heartache, and we look for something everlasting to hold on to. Those who live on the fringes of firm testimony need a transfusion of hope and faith and belief. Hope has its own proclamation: "He is not here: for he is risen, as he said" (Matthew 28:6). Faith has its anthem: "I know that my Redeemer lives" (*Hymns,* no. 136). And belief has its scripture: "Redemption cometh in and through the Holy Messiah; for he is full of grace and truth. . . . and they that believe in him shall be saved" (2 Nephi 2:6–9). Vibrant, living faith and hope become, in process of time, sure knowledge and deep conversion as we proceed along the strait and narrow pathway the Lord has outlined (2 Nephi 31; Alma 32).

JUNE 14

But he knoweth the way that I take:
when he hath tried me, I shall come forth as gold.
JOB 23:10

In the parable of the talents, the Lord teaches us the law of the harvest: We reap what we sow, both temporally and spiritually. What greater joy could we receive than to hear the Lord say, "Well done, good and faithful servant; thou hast been faithful over a few things, I will make thee ruler over many things: enter thou into the joy of thy Lord" (Matthew 25:23). The Old Testament provides a similar lesson in faithfulness in the story of Job, who lived with integrity and faithfulness. Job remained steadfast and immovable even in the midst of severe buffeting: "My foot hath held his steps, his way have I kept, and not declined" (Job 23:11). How reassuring to know that when we are faithful despite life's trials, when we walk with integrity and truly do our best, our "few things" will be added upon, and we will enter into the joy of the Lord.

JUNE 15

Till I die I will not remove mine integrity from me. My righteousness I hold fast, and will not let it go.

Job 27:5–6

Those who have integrity live with a whole and complete heart. They have no secret places, no hypocrisy—what you see is what you get. Such individuals strive daily to choose the right and choose it for the right reasons. They have fused right actions with pure motives. They act out of love rather than for outward appearance. They show their family the same courtesies and respect they show acquaintances and strangers. They uphold sacred truths regardless of circumstance. This "integrity of . . . heart" (D&C 124:15) keeps them faithful and strong even when surrounded by a world of temptation and difficulty. Like Job, no matter what, they persevere in righteousness and testimony. People with integrity know that life is a process of growth. They find the strength to change, because they "[love] that which is right" (D&C124:15). They learn from shortcomings, ask forgiveness, and cleave unwaveringly to truth.

JUNE 16

Behold, the fear of the Lord, that is wisdom; and to depart from evil is understanding.
JOB 28:28

Job teaches us that wisdom cannot be purchased and integrity is not for sale. To the questions "Where shall wisdom be found? and where is the place of understanding?" (Job 28:12), Job learned timeless answers: Reverence for the Lord and his unfathomable ways is wisdom (Isaiah 55:8–9); shunning evil and looking to God as the standard of righteousness is understanding. Job came to know that "the price of wisdom is above rubies" (Job 28:18). Like Nephi, he knew that though we may not know the meaning of all things, we know God loves us (1 Nephi 11:17). It is through experience—trials and tribulations—that we learn the true meaning of life. With Job, we learn that suffering and loss come to all and that affliction may be for experience, discipline, and instruction (D&C 122:1–9). We gain wisdom in coming to understand that unfailing faith in the Redeemer gives us peace in this life and eternal life in the world to come (D&C 59:23).

JUNE 17

Let me be weighed in an even balance, that God may know mine integrity.

Job 31:6

Living a life of integrity means that we live truthfully. What we believe is reflected in who we are: how we think, act, and interact. Living truthfully invites deep trust, abiding love, and inner peace. People with integrity are honest and sincere. They do the right thing when nobody is watching. They keep their word, and they keep confidences. They repay their debts and honor commitments. They accept responsibility for their actions and are dependable in their duties. Of course, we all make mistakes and fall short. But people with integrity know that life is a process of growth. They find the courage to change, because they "[love] that which is right" (D&C 124:15). Integrity begins with faith and is maintained with prayer. Integrity encompasses all of the other virtues. If we have integrity of heart, then we will have all the other virtues.

JUNE 18

Hearken unto this, O Job: stand still,
and consider the wondrous works of God.
JOB 37:14

Oftentimes, in the rush of daily events and the self-interest that occupies much of our time, we fail to pause and in quiet awe look about us at the majesty and magnificence of God's creations. In all ages past and on to our day, the Lord wants us to acknowledge his merciful and powerful hand in all things. Alma, speaking to Korihor the Antichrist, testified that "all things denote there is a God; yea, even the earth, and all things that are upon the face of it, yea, and its motion, yea, and also all the planets which move in their regular form do witness that there is a Supreme Creator" (Alma 30:44). To know and worship the Lord, we must be still, listen to the inner voice that whispers comfort and peace, and with hearts full of gratitude ponder "the wondrous works of him which is perfect in knowledge" (Job 37:16).

Where wast thou when I laid the foundations of the earth? declare, if thou hast understanding. When the morning stars sang together, and all the sons of God shouted for joy?

JOB 38:4, 7

With the restored knowledge of a premortal existence, Latter-day Saints read Job 38:4, 7 with a special understanding: We believe these verses refer to our joyous response to the presentation of God's plan of salvation in the premortal councils. And yet there is another meaning to this passage. Job's relationship with the Lord was such that he almost seemed to question God's mode of operation—why He did what He did. God essentially responds to Job by asking: "Are you really in a position to ask such questions? Is your mind capable of comprehending the works and ways of the Infinite? Can you fathom the plans and purposes and pursuits of a perfect Being?" Such rhetorical questions were intended to humble Job, to remind him of who God is and who man is. We cannot, from our limited mortal perspective, grasp the enormous scope of the challenge our Father in Heaven faces in orchestrating the lives of humankind. How, then, do we dare question his wisdom?

JUNE 20

Depart from me, all ye workers of iniquity.

Psalm 6:8

Toward the end of the Sermon on the Mount, the Savior addressed the first part of Psalm 6:8 to at least two groups: those who did not choose to do the will of our Heavenly Father while on earth, and those who had done what most of us would consider works of righteousness but who had never performed the most sacred of all assignments—namely, coming to know the Lord. It is not enough just to know *about* the Lord. The sober warning is ever before us: Those who profess righteousness but have not drawn close to the Lord of Life will receive the Savior's censure: "I never knew you: Depart from me, ye that work iniquity." Such persons who do not know their Master cannot associate with him everlastingly (Matthew 7:21–23; compare JST; Mosiah 26:27).

JUNE 21

What is man, that thou art mindful of him?. . .
For thou hast made him a little lower than the angels, and
hast crowned him with glory and honour.

PSALM 8:4–5

Each of us is a beloved spirit son or daughter of God. As our eternal Father, he looks upon us with perfect love and has put in place a plan for our divine destiny and ultimate happiness. All who walk the earth have kept their first estate and are here to prove themselves "to see if they will do all things whatsoever the Lord their God shall command them" (Abraham 3:25). Those who obey the fulness of the gospel law during their second estate will inherit the "greatest of all the gifts of God," even eternal life (D&C 14:7; 29:43–44). Eternal life is the quality of life that God himself enjoys. Thus, those who gain eternal life receive exaltation and the fulness of the Father (D&C 132:19–20).

JUNE 22

For thou hast made him a little lower than the angels.

PSALM 8:5

The message of Psalm 8:5 is beautiful as it reads in the King James Version—the nobility and premier place of mankind as the crown of God's creation. But beneath the surface there is more. The Hebrew for the phrase "a little lower than the angels" actually reads "a little lower than the *Elohim,*" meaning the Gods. Because of the fear in Christendom and in other world religions that men and women should dare in some way defy the Creator/creature chasm, people have chosen to believe that man is of a different species, of a lower order, than the Almighty. The Prophet Joseph Smith boldly declared that while God our Heavenly Father is infinite and eternal, he may be comprehended and approached, and we may eventually, through the love and mercy of our Savior, acquire many of his divine attributes and powers.

JUNE 23

The fool hath said in his heart, There is no God.

PSALM 14:1

It is indeed unwise to declare that there is no God. The truth is, it takes more effort to be an atheist than to be a believer in God. Too many things, including the order of the cosmos and the signs and symbols of nature, attest to the benevolent hand and gracious work of an all-wise Creator. In his inspired translation of this passage, the Prophet Joseph Smith added a detail that highlighted the depth of misunderstanding, even among those who believe in God: "The fool hath said in his heart, There is no man that hath seen God" (JST Psalm 14:1). Foolishness comes in many forms, including the false notion that God has not revealed himself face to face, particularly to his covenant spokesmen, the prophets. The Restoration offers a divine corrective: God has appeared, has spoken, and will continue to appear and speak as long as time shall last and the earth shall stand, according to the faith of the children of men.

JUNE 24

For thou wilt not leave my soul in hell;
neither wilt thou suffer thine Holy One to see corruption.
PSALM 16:10

Psalm 16:10 has a dual meaning, for it is a messianic psalm. Because of David's immorality, complicated by his scheme to commit murder, he fell from grace and lost his exaltation (D&C 132:39). He did receive the assurance, however, that his soul would not be left in hell; that is, he would eventually come forth in the resurrection to a kingdom of glory. The Savior had the same promise. His spirit would come forth from the postmortal spirit world after three days in the tomb, and thus his body would not be allowed to decompose or to know corruption. Jesus was not left in *Sheol* (Hebrew) or *Hades* (Greek), in the world of the departed. Rather, after he had taught the gospel to the faithful and organized his righteous forces, he came forth in resurrected glory, thus assuring the same for you and me.

JUNE 25

The law of the Lord is perfect, converting the soul.

PSALM 19:7

Our Heavenly Father delights in the happiness of his children. He is an exalted, glorified "Man of Holiness" (Moses 6:57), and he is happy. He wants his children to possess what he possesses, and so he gives commandments and laws to bless our lives, to bring happiness to us, not to provide roadblocks to fun or impediments to our enjoyment. His celestial structure enables us to walk the straight and narrow path that leads to life eternal and thus to avoid the wide way that leads to destruction and misery. Those who come unto God and seek to bring to pass his purposes are "crowned with blessings from above, yea, and with commandments not a few" (D&C 59:4).

JUNE 26

The testimony of the Lord is sure, making wise the simple.

PSALM 19:7

There are few things more precious in this life than a witness, borne of the Spirit, that God lives, that Jesus Christ is the Savior and Redeemer, and that God has spoken anew in our day through modern prophets. When we possess such a spiritual assurance, we possess a testimony. Such a knowledge is from heaven, and it is sure and certain. Such a knowledge makes the simplest of us wise pertaining to things of eternity. Such a knowledge empowers us to face the storms of life and the turmoils of our telestial tenement.

JUNE 27

The fear of the Lord is clean, enduring for ever.

PSALM 19:9

The Psalmist teaches us that "the fear of the Lord is the beginning of wisdom" (Psalm 111:10). The prophetic refrain is clear: We should fear God and give glory to him. But this fear is not the fear the world knows, one in which we shudder and tremble in anxiety and anticipation of wrath. Rather, to fear the Lord is to reverence him, to respect him, to look to him as the fountain of all light and love and truth, the source of all that is good and uplifting. In short, to fear God is to humble ourselves before him—to acknowledge his greatness and majesty, to confess our weakness, to plead for his mercy and grace.

JUNE 28

My God, my God, why hast thou forsaken me?
PSALM 22:1

Once again, we encounter in Psalm 22 a messianic psalm that has dual application. Having sinned against light and understanding, King David has lost the guiding and comforting influence of the Holy Spirit and stands alone and naked in his wickedness. There is nothing quite so painful as the alienation known only to those who have walked and talked in the light of the Spirit and then transgressed the laws of God and lost that sacred influence. While on the cross in the meridian of time, suffering incomprehensible pain, the Savior experienced once again all of the agonies of Gethsemane, including the agony associated with the loss of the Father's sustaining Spirit. Our Lord thereby became, as the apostle Paul declared, "sin for us," that we might gain the "righteousness of God" through him (2 Corinthians 5:21).

JUNE 29

Yea, though I walk through the valley of the shadow of death, I will fear no evil: for thou art with me; thy rod and thy staff they comfort me.

PSALM 23:4

All of us face difficulty and heartache as we walk through life. And every person born into mortality will in due course walk into the valley of death. Were it not for a succoring Lord and the glorious gospel plan, life's trials and ultimate end could fill us with trepidation and despair. But Jesus will not leave us comfortless, without help and hope. With him beside us we have nothing to fear. The Psalmist praised the Lord for his loving kindness: "Though I walk in the midst of trouble, thou wilt revive me: thou shalt stretch forth thine hand against the wrath of mine enemies, and thy right hand shall save me" (Psalm 138:7). The comforting rod and staff of the Good Shepherd protect and guide his sheep. They are not the aversive tools of an authoritarian monarch but the gentle touch of a loving, watchful caretaker. The Good Shepherd slumbers not as he watches over his faithful flock.

JUNE 30

Surely goodness and mercy shall follow me all the days of my life: and I will dwell in the house of the Lord for ever.

PSALM 23:6

Without question, the Twenty-third Psalm is one of the most beloved and oft-repeated scriptural passages. It is a tribute to the Good Shepherd, the one who loves and leads his sheep in paths of righteousness. It is a sacred statement of his tender promises to those who listen to his voice and follow where he leads. More is intended in verse 6 than appears on the surface. To have goodness and mercy follow us all the days of our life sounds impressive enough, but the meaning from the original language is even stronger. The original implies that God's goodness and mercy will pursue us, entice us, and draw us toward the more abundant life all the time that we are here on earth. The Good Shepherd is as eager to find his sheep as he is for his sheep to find him.

July

Behold, to obey is better than sacrifice,
and to hearken than the fat of rams.

1 Samuel 15:22

JULY 1

The earth is the Lord's, and the fulness thereof; the world, and they that dwell therein.

PSALM 24:1

The Psalmist testifies that the earth and all things that dwell therein are the Lord's. Further, "the heavens are thine, the earth also is thine: as for the world and the fulness thereof, thou hast founded them" (Psalm 89:11). The Lord is King of heaven and earth. Truly, to come to this beautiful planet is a great blessing. We are here to learn and grow, to repent and forgive, to love and serve. As we work to fulfill our divine destiny as sons and daughters of God, we fill the measure of our creation and find joy. The Lord said, "For the earth is full, and there is enough and to spare; yea, I prepared all things, and have given unto the children of men to be agents unto themselves" (D&C 104:17). We become wise stewards as we use the earth's resources wisely, as we respect the wonders of nature, as we treat other people with dignity and kindness. Praise the Lord for his bountiful blessings.

JULY 2

Who shall ascend into the hill of the Lord? or who shall stand in his holy place? He that hath clean hands, and a pure heart; who hath not lifted up his soul unto vanity, nor sworn deceitfully.

PSALM 24:3–4

The temple is a place of sacred instruction and ordinance work, a place of reverence for everlasting things. To enter worthily is our commission as Saints of God. Our desires must be pure and holy as we enter its walls. We must be chaste and clean, striving to keep ourselves unspotted from the world. We must be people of integrity and honest in our dealings. Although we are all less than perfect, the temple is the place to go for those who desire righteousness, spiritual growth, and selfless service. It is the place to go to be taught sacred things, a place of holiness for those striving to become as God would have them become. In the temple all dress the same; there is no rank or status or prestige. Inside temple walls, position, power, and possessions are meaningless. To enter the house of the Lord is to stand on holy ground.

JULY 3

For his anger endureth but a moment; in his favour is life: weeping may endure for a night, but joy cometh in the morning.
PSALM 30:5

Each of us faces poignant, painful moments in life that bring us to our knees and even cause us to wonder why we were born. Perhaps it is the loss of a loved one, the waywardness of a child, the anticipation of death, or even the distress and loneliness associated with sin. We grieve and we sorrow. We long and we yearn for something better. Sleep flees, and we walk the floors at night. God's promise to his people is that one day the tears of this life will be dried, and beauty will replace ashes. "For his anger kindleth against the wicked; they repent, and in a moment it is turned away, and they are in his favour, and he giveth them life; therefore, weeping may endure for a night, but joy cometh in the morning" (JST Psalm 30:5).

JULY 4

O Lord my God, I will give thanks unto thee for ever.

PSALM 30:12

All things at all times—every breath we take, every sunrise and sunset, is a gift from a loving God. Gratitude is absolutely vital for those who seek the Spirit of the Lord and more spirituality in their lives. Without thanksgiving, we deny the power of the Atonement and mock the great plan of happiness. The Savior's condescending to come to earth, to be born among men, and then to suffer and die for us must never be spoken of casually. His atonement is the most sublime and important event in all eternity and must be regarded with reverence and deep appreciation. We speak of the Savior with respect and thankfulness, with meekness and devotion. We feel like Nephi of old, who soulfully confessed, "My heart doth magnify his holy name" (2 Nephi 25:13). We echo and never forget the words of David: "I will give thanks unto thee for ever" (Psalm 30:12).

JULY 5

O love the Lord, all ye his saints: for the Lord preserveth the faithful. . . . Be of good courage, and he shall strengthen your heart.

PSALM 31:23–24

The Lord will strengthen and preserve his humble followers. He wants us to succeed, to press forward with faith, and to obey his commandments so that we can inherit all that he has (Revelation 21:7). He wants us to bless others with our service. President Gordon B. Hinckley said: "We all worry about our performance. We all wish we could do better. But unfortunately we do not realize, we do not often see the results that come of what we do. . . . You are doing the best you can, and that best results in good to yourself and to others. Do not nag yourself with a sense of failure. Get on your knees and ask for the blessings of the Lord; then stand on your feet and do what you are asked to do. Then leave the matter in the hands of the Lord. You will discover that you have accomplished something beyond price" (*Ensign,* November 2003, 113–14). We love the Lord best by following him (John 14:15).

Blessed is he whose transgression is forgiven, whose sin is covered.

PSALM 32:1

As is well known, *atonement* is created from three English words—*at-one-ment.* The Hebrew word translated as "atone" is the word *kafar,* which means "to forgive or to cover." Through the atonement of Jesus Christ, our sins are covered, much as we would use a cloth to cover a table. In addition, our sins are covered in the same way that one friend might say to another after lunch when the bill is presented, "I'll cover it." When Jesus said, "It is finished" (John 19:30) he was announcing that he had completed his earthly mission, had finished the work he had been sent to do in this second estate. The one Greek word that is translated "it is finished" means, literally, "paid in full." The purchase was made, the redemption was accomplished, the debts were covered, and thereby salvation came to the repentant.

Blessed is the man unto whom the Lord imputeth not iniquity, and in whose spirit there is no guile.

PSALM 32:2

We seldom use the word *impute* in modern conversation, but it is a significant theological term. To impute is to credit, to put on an account. When Jesus suffered in Gethsemane and on Golgotha for the sins of all humankind, in a way that is incomprehensible to us, the burden and weight of the sins of humanity were imputed to our Lord. That is, it was as though Jesus had become the great sinner, as though he had inherited the world's curse (2 Corinthians 5:21; Galatians 3:13). Conversely, through coming unto Christ by faith and repentance, his righteousness is imputed to us. That is, it is as though we possessed the full righteousness and perfection of our Lord and Master. Jesus was not guilty of sin, but sin was imputed to him. We are not as righteous as Jesus, but through his perfect atonement and our repentance, his righteousness may be imputed to us. Thank God for the great exchange.

JULY 8

Blessed is the nation whose God is the Lord; and the people whom he hath chosen for his own inheritance.

PSALM 33:12

Nations stand or fall according to the degree to which they look to God for life. Modern revelation tells us, for example, that this nation was foreordained by God to serve a divine purpose—namely, the restoration of the fulness of the everlasting gospel. Consequently, wise men and women were raised up to serve as the founders of the nation that would serve as the headquarters of the Zion of God (D&C 101:80). What is true of America is true of all nations: If its inhabitants forget God and travel in wayward paths, they are left unto themselves to inherit that which could have been avoided. In speaking of this land, Moroni decreed: "Behold, this is a choice land, and whatsoever nation shall possess it shall be free from bondage, and from captivity, and from all other nations under heaven, if they will but serve the God of the land, who is Jesus Christ" (Ether 2:12).

JULY 9

The Lord is nigh unto them that are of a broken heart; and saveth such as be of a contrite spirit.

PSALM 34:18

Cynicism, skepticism, and sin harden our hearts; they make it difficult for us to sense the mind and will of God and things of righteousness. A hardened heart must be either softened or broken. If we turn regularly to the Almighty and plead in prayer for a divine perspective, the Lord will soften us and enable us to have believing hearts (1 Nephi 2:16). When we repent properly and possess godly sorrow for sin, we experience a broken heart, a sobering realization of what we have done, a solemn reminder of him against whom we have sinned. A contrite spirit is a humbled spirit, a will that is yielded to a greater will. Since the time of the great and last sacrifice, we are called upon to make an offering of a broken heart and a contrite spirit (3 Nephi 9:19–20). In short, we are charged to yield our hearts to God (Helaman 3:35).

Fret not thyself because of evil-doers,
neither be thou envious against the workers of iniquity.
PSALM 37:1

We do not take counsel from our fears and thus do not occupy our minds with the world and worldliness. Rather, we take seriously the counsel of the apostle Paul: "Whatsoever things are true, whatsoever things are honest, whatsoever things are just, whatsoever things are pure, whatsoever things are lovely, whatsoever things are of good report; if there be any virtue, and if there be any praise, think on these things" (Philippians 4:8; Articles of Faith 1:13). We have no reason to envy the workers of iniquity. Not only are their holdings temporary but their fate is not to be desired. Through the eye of faith we see that many things that charm us in this fallen world simply will not pass through celestial customs. Further, one whose eye is single to the glory of God comes to be filled with light, comes to know all things, and eventually becomes an inheritor of all things. What have we to envy?

JULY 11

Cease from anger, and forsake wrath.
Psalm 37:8

Anger is a damaging corrosive that simply does not work. It tends to elicit more anger, more resentment, more contention. It may seem to help in the short run, but long term it is counterproductive, creating more problems than it solves. Anger makes people more rigid, less thoughtful, and less capable of having positive relationships. Anger hardens hearts, creating feelings of bitterness and animosity that often echo down the generations. The Lord's way is to put off anger, wrath, and malice (Colossians 3:8); it is long-suffering and gentleness, meekness and love unfeigned (D&C 121:41). Charity, pure love—the opposite of anger—"suffereth long, and is kind; . . . charity vaunteth not itself, is not puffed up, doth not behave itself unseemly, seeketh not her own, is not easily provoked, thinketh no evil" (1 Corinthians 13:4–5). The Lord's way is the pathway to peace and joy.

JULY 12

But the meek shall inherit the earth; and shall delight themselves in the abundance of peace.

PSALM 37:11

Jesus quoted the first part of Psalm 37:11 as one of his Beatitudes in the Sermon on the Mount (Matthew 5:5). It is a Beatitude filled with irony, for the meek person is one who is in control of his or her emotions, one who demonstrates poise under provocation. "In a world too preoccupied with winning through intimidation and seeking to be number one," President Howard W. Hunter reminded us, "no large crowd is standing in line to buy books that call for mere meekness. But the meek shall inherit the earth, a pretty impressive corporate takeover—and done *without* intimidation! Sooner or later, and we pray sooner *than* later, everyone will acknowledge that Christ's way is not only the *right* way, but ultimately the *only* way to hope and joy" (*That We Might Have Joy,* 9). Indeed, it is the meek, those who have dispelled the noise within themselves, who will know peace forevermore.

JULY 13

The steps of a good man are ordered by the Lord: and he delighteth in his way. Though he fall, he shall not be utterly cast down: for the Lord upholdeth him with his hand.

PSALM 37:23–24

Each of us possesses moral agency (D&C 101:78), and we have the capacity, through our choices, to determine our destiny. On the other hand, our Heavenly Father is as intimately involved in our lives as we will allow him to be, as closely tied to our daily walk and talk as we permit him to be. Who would not delight in being led and encouraged and empowered along the path of life by One who knows the end from the beginning and can counsel us with perfect knowledge? One great sign of spiritual maturity is the extent to which we strive to be led by the Spirit. When we leave the light momentarily, we feel abhorrence with the darkness, repent quickly (D&C 109:21), and move back into the light. May it be true of us as it was of Oliver Granger: "When he falls he shall rise again, for his sacrifice shall be more sacred unto me than his increase" (D&C 117:13).

JULY 14

I will declare mine iniquity; I will be sorry for my sin.

PSALM 38:18

Godly sorrow for sin and a heartfelt desire to confess and forsake are the building blocks of the path to peace and joy. But we must not only sorrow and desire—we must act. "You can cast out guilt, overcome depression, receive the blessing of peace of mind, and find enduring joy," counseled Elder Richard G. Scott. "Pray for help and guidance, and you will be led to find it. Go to where you know the light of truth shines—to a worthy friend, a loving bishop or stake president, an understanding parent. Please come back. We love you. We need you. Follow the path to peace and joy through complete repentance. The Savior will help you obtain forgiveness as you sincerely follow all of the steps to repentance. He is the Redeemer. He loves you. He wants you to have peace and joy in your life" (*Ensign,* November 2000, 27). Everlasting happiness is found in the forgiveness that comes of the Savior's infinite atonement.

JULY 15

Lord, make me to know mine end, and the measure of my days, what it is; that I may know how frail I am.

PSALM 39:4

As we draw closer to our Heavenly Father, we also come to know ourselves better. The Prophet Joseph Smith taught that "if men do not comprehend the character of God, they do not comprehend themselves" (*Teachings,* 343). Increased sensitivity to the Spirit leads to an ever-increasing awareness of who we are, Whose we are, and why we are here on earth. It also leads us to a more poignant grasp of God's holiness and our own weakness. Such an understanding humbles us, emphasizes our limitations, and points us ever so powerfully to Him who has no limitations. As Paul and Moroni taught, when we confess our weakness, we are opening ourselves to divine empowerment and strength (2 Corinthians 12:9–10; Ether 12:27).

JULY 16

I waited patiently for the Lord. . . . He brought me up also out of an horrible pit, out of the miry clay, and set my feet upon a rock.

PSALM 40:1–2

The Lord and his infinite atonement provide the means of escape from the depressing pits and miserable molehills of life. All believers wait, as did the Psalmist of old, for the messianic moment of rescue and redemption. Amulek taught the compelling need for the atonement of Jesus Christ: "It is expedient that an atonement should be made; for according to the great plan of the Eternal God there must be an atonement made, or else all mankind must unavoidably perish" (Alma 34:9). Were there no atonement, we would be forever mired in the mud and muck of life—with no chance of rescue; were there no atonement, we would be forever lost in desperation and despair—with no hope of release (2 Nephi 9:8–9, 26). Only in the Lord can we find rest to our souls (Matthew 11:29). Only by doing the works of righteousness can we find peace in this life and eternal life in the world to come (D&C 59:23).

JULY 17

Be still, and know that I am God.

Psalm 46:10

The faithful through the ages have been reassured by the words "Be still, and know that I am God" (Psalm 46:10). Even when hope seems lost, the Lord will not leave us comfortless. In our trials we can hold onto these consoling words and know that God is watching over us. Although we may not understand all things, we know that the Lord loves us and will not forsake us (1 Nephi 11:17). In 1833 the Saints suffered intense persecution as mobs drove them from their homes, destroyed crops, seized possessions, and dealt out violence and threats of death. But the Lord did not leave his people comfortless: "Let your hearts be comforted concerning Zion; for all flesh is in mine hands; be still and know that I am God" (D&C 101:16). We will have our challenges, our heartaches and trials, but God lives, he knows and loves us, and he has created a great plan of happiness for our well-being and joy.

JULY 18

Gather my Saints together unto me;
those that have made a covenant with me by sacrifice.
PSALM 50:5

We gather with the Saints when we enter into a covenant relationship with Christ and congregate in the stakes of Zion. We gather as we hold back the world and come together in righteousness to strengthen one another. As we turn our hearts to heaven and our thoughts to everlasting things, we gather with the Saints. Our devotion to the gospel covenant is manifest in our willingness to offer all—our time, means, energy, everything that we possess—to build up the kingdom of God on the earth. We stand on the shoulders of covenant-keeping giants who have sacrificed much so that we may enjoy the blessings of the gospel today. Our sacrifice will not come from pushing a handcart across a frozen highland, but it nonetheless will come from the same place—our consecrated hearts. As we faithfully follow the Lord and his authorized servants and as we gather with the Saints, our heartfelt covenant is steadfast and sure.

JULY 19

Against thee, thee only, have I sinned, and done this evil in thy sight: that thou mightest be justified when thou speakest, and be clear when thou judgest.

PSALM 51:4

King David's heart-wrenching prayer affirms that there is no such thing as private sin. It is vanity and foolishness to suppose that "I'm not hurting anyone but myself." Not only do our missteps bring pain and distress to friends, family, and loved ones, but, more important, they are committed against the One who loves us the most; they are committed directly against our God. As Jehovah explained to Samuel when the Israelites rejected prophetic counsel, "They have not rejected thee, but they have rejected me, that I should not reign over them" (1 Samuel 8:7). This is why complete repentance must always involve confession of our sins to our Father in Heaven as well as to those against whom we have sinned.

Behold, I was shapen in iniquity;
and in sin did my mother conceive me.
PSALM 51:5

In Psalm 51 the fallen King David, in agony over his sins, described the state of unredeemed humanity. Because the Latter-day Saint view of the Fall is much more optimistic than that which is taught throughout Christendom—from the revealed truth that our first parents went into the Garden of Eden to fall, that their transgression was a part of the Father's plan, and that it was forgiven through the blood of the Redeemer (2 Nephi 2:25; Moses 6:53)—we sometimes forget that the Fall does indeed affect all forms of life. Although we are not accountable for Adam and Eve's transgression, we are certainly affected by it, both physically and spiritually. We are "conceived in sin" (Moses 6:55) in that we are born into a world of sin. Conception is the means whereby a fallen nature—mortality, the flesh—is transmitted to the posterity of Adam and Eve. We are thus in desperate need of redemption and deliverance, which the infinite atonement affords us.

JULY 21

Create in me a clean heart, O God;
and renew a right spirit within me.
PSALM 51:10

We are made pure after repentance for sin only when our hearts have been cleansed and renewed through the blood of Christ and the medium of the sanctifier, the Holy Ghost. Behavioral modification is not sufficient. Learning new skills is not sufficient. Acting more appropriately is not sufficient. For lasting change to occur, especially in the wake of serious sin, we must undergo what the Book of Mormon prophets called a "mighty change" of heart, a change that takes place from the inside out (Alma 5:12). Eventually "we have no more disposition to do evil, but to do good continually" (Mosiah 5:2). We cannot then "look upon sin save it were with abhorrence" (Alma 13:12). Such a change is a rebirth of the soul, a transition into the realm of righteousness.

JULY 22

Cast thy burden upon the Lord, and he shall sustain thee.

PSALM 55:22

The Lord will sustain us as we turn to him with full purpose of heart. He said, "Come unto me, all ye that labour and are heavy laden, and I will give you rest. Take my yoke upon you, and learn of me; for I am meek and lowly in heart: and ye shall find rest unto your souls. For my yoke is easy, and my burden is light" (Matthew 11:28–30). Those words resonate in the hearts of all who worry, all who are burdened in some way, all who face challenges and disappointment. Life is difficult. No one gets through it without experiencing heartache, pain, or discontent. Look into anyone's heart, and you will find some cause for sorrow. But with the anguish comes the promise of peace. With the despair comes the hope of happiness. It is faith in the Lord that gives us peace and hope. It is in turning to him, believing him, following him, that we find lasting happiness.

JULY 23

In God I will praise his word, in God I have put my trust; I will not fear what flesh can do unto me.

PSALM 56:4

If we trust the Lord, we have nothing to fear. As the Psalmist said, "The Lord is on my side; I will not fear: what can man do unto me?" (Psalm 118:6). That does not mean we will not have setbacks and sorrows, disappointments and difficulties. We will. But we rise above our trials through our trust in the Lord—we rely on his love and redemption; we put our faith and hope in him. The Lord assured the Prophet Joseph while he was held captive in the dark and depressing Liberty Jail: "Therefore, hold on thy way. . . . Thy days are known, and thy years shall not be numbered less; therefore, fear not what man can do, for God shall be with you forever and ever" (D&C 122:9). When we fully turn to the Lord, he will not turn away. If we truly put our trust in him, he will comfort and bless us with his enabling power.

JULY 24

In God is my salvation and my glory: the rock of my strength, and my refuge, is in God. Trust in him at all times.
PSALM 62:7–8

We live in a world of difficulty and heartache. At times it seems that we can't go on, that life is without any joy or rejoicing. All of it—the good and the bad, the bitter and the sweet—provides opportunities to develop and manifest our faithfulness. "The test a loving God has set before us is not to see if we can endure difficulty. It is to see if we can endure it well," said Elder Henry B. Eyring. "We pass the test by showing that we remembered Him and the commandments He gave us. And to endure well is to keep those commandments whatever the opposition, whatever the temptation, and whatever the tumult around us. We have that clear understanding because the restored gospel makes the plan of happiness so plain" (*Ensign,* May 2004, 17). In our tutoring trials, we can learn more about the things of eternity and prepare our hearts for eternal life, which is God's greatest gift (D&C 14:7).

JULY 25

I have said, Ye are gods; and
all of you are children of the most High.
PSALM 82:6

All human beings—male and female—are created in the image of God. Each is a beloved spirit son or daughter of heavenly parents, and, as such, each has a divine nature and destiny" ("The Family: A Proclamation," *Ensign,* November 1995, 102). We are children of God, who has sent us here to learn of him and to grow in light and truth as we develop the attributes of godliness. "No greater ideal has been revealed than the supernal truth that we are the children of God, and we differ, by virtue of our creation, from all other living things," said Elder Boyd K. Packer. "No idea has been more destructive of happiness, no philosophy has produced more sorrow, more heartbreak and mischief; no ideal has done more to destroy the family than the idea that we are not the offspring of God, only advanced animals, compelled to yield to every carnal urge" (*Ensign,* May 1992, 67). God, our Father, wants us to know who we truly are.

JULY 26

Truth shall spring out of the earth;
and righteousness shall look down from heaven.
PSALM 85:11

Verse 11 of Psalm 85 is but a small part of a larger prophecy of the work we know as the Restoration: a glimpse of the First Vision, the coming forth of the Book of Mormon and its expansive role, and the establishment of the center stake of Zion. In his inspired translation of Genesis, the Prophet Joseph wrote the words of God to Enoch: "And righteousness will I send down out of heaven; and truth will I send forth out of the earth, to bear testimony of mine Only Begotten; his resurrection from the dead; yea, and also the resurrection of all men; and righteousness and truth will I cause to sweep the earth as with a flood, to gather out mine elect from the four quarters of the earth, unto a place which I shall prepare, an Holy City, . . . and it shall be called Zion, a New Jerusalem" (Moses 7:62).

O come, let us worship and bow down:
let us kneel before the Lord our maker.
PSALM 95:6

True worship is an expression of reverence for the Creator: "For he is our God; and we are the people of his pasture, and the sheep of his hand" (Psalm 95:6). Worship is respect and devotion to the Most High. It is honoring his name by keeping it holy and placing no one ahead of him in our affections (Exodus 20:3–7). It is living in such a way that integrity and humility guide our actions and interactions with others. President Gordon B. Hinckley said: "Let the pulpits of all the churches ring with righteousness. Let people everywhere bow in reverence before the Almighty who is our one true strength. Let us look inward and adjust our priorities and standards. Let us look outward in the spirit of the Golden Rule" (*Teachings of Gordon B. Hinckley,* 493). True worship is a daily reflection of an inner conversion—manifest not only in words and intentions but in attitudes and actions.

JULY 28

The Lord hath sworn, and will not repent,
Thou art a priest for ever after the order of Melchizedek.
PSALM 110:4

Jesus Christ was and is and will be forevermore the great "High Priest of our profession" (Hebrews 3:1). Because he did what he was sent here to do, because he carried out the will of the Father in every particular, and because he kept the covenant of the Melchizedek Priesthood, God swore unto him with an oath that he would be a high priest forever, reigning among the just as King of kings and Lord of lords. God swore the same oath to such ancient prophets as Enoch and Melchizedek (JST Genesis 14:25–40), just as he will to every faithful elder of the kingdom who magnifies his callings in the priesthood, gives diligent heed to the words of eternal life, receives the Lord's servants, and lives by every word of God (D&C 84:33–44). Truly, all who qualify for the fulness of priesthood blessings "are made like unto the Son of God, abiding a priest continually" (JST Hebrews 7:3).

JULY 29

O praise the Lord, all ye nations: praise him, all ye people. For his merciful kindness is great toward us: and the truth of the Lord endureth for ever.

PSALM 117:1–2

The Psalms provide an exceptional literature of worship, and their most prominent feature is praise. "Praise the Lord" is the acclamation that reverberates from Psalm 1 to Psalm 150. Singing, dancing, rejoicing, adoring—all are the language of praise. Accompanying praise is thanksgiving. As we praise, we give thanks to the Lord for his loving-kindness and his mercy and grace, and we acknowledge his hand in all things. We praise and give thanks for his perfect life, his perfect truth. We praise and give thanks for the gospel plan of happiness, for blessings large and small, for life and love. We manifest our genuine praise and authentic thankfulness to the Lord in the daily walk and talk of our lives. He is the Lord of all nations, of all people. He is the way, the truth, and the life, the means by which we come unto the Father (John 14:6).

JULY 30

The stone which the builders refused
is become the head stone of the corner.
PSALM 118:22

There is a legend among the Jews that at the time of the building of Solomon's temple the master builders discarded, by mistake, the cornerstone of the sacred edifice. The Psalmist drew upon that legend, as did the Savior himself (Matthew 21:42). It is an ironic type of meridian Jewry. Jacob, son of Lehi, wrote, "By the stumbling of the Jews they will reject the stone upon which they might build and have safe foundation. But behold, according to the scriptures, this stone shall become the great, and the last, and the only sure foundation, upon which the Jews can build" (Jacob 4:15–16; compare Helaman 5:12). Nonetheless, the Almighty has provided, in a grand and mysterious manner, a means by which the Jews can once again build their lives upon him who is the Chief Cornerstone (1 Nephi 15:15; Jacob 4:17–5:77; Ephesians 2:19–20; 1 Corinthians 3:11).

JULY 31

I have chosen the way of truth. . . .
I have stuck unto thy testimonies.
PSALM 119:30–31

Parents have a sacred responsibility to rear their children in love and righteousness, to exemplify by precept and by example the transforming principles of the restored gospel. Yet we are free to choose how we will respond to the message of salvation. President Gordon B. Hinckley said: "I believe this to be the most marvelous age in all the history of the world . . . when there is such a great flowering of knowledge. What a tragedy it is, what a bleak and terrible thing to witness a son or daughter on whom you counted so much walk the tortuous path that leads down to hell. On the other hand, what a glorious and beautiful thing it is to see the child of your dreams walk with head up, standing tall, unafraid, and with confidence, taking advantage of the tremendous opportunities that open around him or her" (*Ensign,* November 2000, 52). May we choose the way of testimony and truth.

August

Fear not: for they that be with us
are more than they that be with them.
2 Kings 6:16

AUGUST 1

Behold, he that keepeth Israel shall
neither slumber nor sleep. The Lord is thy keeper.
PSALM 121:4–5

The process of spiritual growth can be long and hard, yet it can also be joyful. It takes time for the seed of faith and testimony to take root, sprout, and then blossom. When we exercise faith in the Lord and seek righteousness, we have hope in the future and power in the present. Victor Hugo advised, "Have courage for the great sorrows of life, and patience for the small ones; and when you have laboriously accomplished your daily task, go to sleep in peace. God is awake" (*Richard L. Evans Quote Book,* 139). No matter how tired we may be or how weary our efforts become, God is watching over us. He is our loving Father, our keeper and caretaker as we journey life's challenging pathways. With the wide-angle viewfinder of faith, we have the eternal perspective to know that we owe God our lives, our souls, the very air we breathe. We walk the road of life with faith and peace, knowing God is awake.

AUGUST 2

Children are an heritage of the Lord.

PSALM 127:3

Psalm 127:3 is the only passage of scripture quoted in "The Family: A Proclamation to the World" (*Ensign,* November 1995, 102). It reflects the importance the Lord places on the sacred duty of parents to love and care for their children. All children come from God, the Eternal Father, as well as from a human father and mother, and so they have spiritual and eternal parentage as well as earthly. Human parents thus have a stewardship relationship with their children, rather than an ownership relationship. Parents are entrusted for a season with a precious child to rear in love and righteousness, to teach in the way of the Lord, to provide for and protect and nurture. Parents will be accountable to God for their efforts (D&C 68:25). As a heritage of God, children are entitled to his fullest blessings—to become "joint-heirs with Christ" (Romans 8:17).

AUGUST 3

As arrows are in the hand of a mighty man; so are children of the youth. Happy is the man that hath his quiver full of them.
PSALM 127:4–5

Those who have the great privilege of parenthood are truly blessed. They are part of a sacred stewardship to rear their children in love and righteousness and set for them an example worthy of emulation. Theirs is a both a serious responsibility and a joyful adventure to do all they can to raise a happy, well-adjusted, and righteous generation. Those who want the best for their sons and daughters, want for them meekness and mercy more than money, love and patience more than power, compassion and submissiveness more than status. And there are those who parent all their lives who are never birth-parents themselves—they reach out in love and kindness to other children, they fulfill callings that bless the youth, they manifest goodness in their community as they serve and work to bless children all around them. Happy is the person who loves and serves children.

AUGUST 4

Out of the depths have I cried unto thee, O Lord. Lord, hear my voice: let thine ears be attentive to the voice of my supplications.

PSALM 130:1–2

Who has not cried out in the depths of affliction for the comforting hand of the Lord? In all times and places, we have supplicated heaven's help in the trials of life. We plead with the Lord to sustain us, to succor us, to soften our hearts as we journey through life. To be without the influence of the Spirit, to feel that the Lord's listening ear is closed to our petitions, causes the deepest personal despair. But hope, help, and healing are found in the Lord. Our anguish can be turned into sincere submission and patient pleading as we seek the Lord. Our heartache can be turned into the kind of resolute faith and true conversion that are fired only in the furnace of affliction. The trials we endure well build our faith in everlasting things and give us confidence and strength in the Lord. The Lord will surely hear our voice as we cleave unto him with all our heart (D&C 11:19).

AUGUST 5

I will worship toward thy holy temple, and praise thy name for thy lovingkindness and for thy truth.

PSALM 138:2

Anciently, the faithful frequently prayed toward the temple—they literally faced in the direction where the house of the Lord was. This practice served as a constant reminder of God's love for his chosen people, his presence among them, and his willingness to manifest himself in holy places. In our day we may not turn ourselves literally toward the temple when we pray, but the temple remains the focal point, the center, of the society of Zion. The temple stands as an eternal link, connecting past, present, and future; time and eternity; the heavens and the earth; husbands and wives; parents and children; and men and women to Christ and the Father. We turn to the temple inasmuch as the temple is the high point of our holy commonwealth, the final phase of gathering, the consummate end toward which all other means among the people of God point.

AUGUST 6

Search me, O God, and know my heart:
try me, and know my thoughts: and see if there be any wicked way in me, and lead me in the way everlasting.
PSALM 139:23–24

God knows where we are headed, both here and hereafter, because he knows what is in our heart and head in the present. This life is a time of probation and proving, of testing and trial. We are here to prove ourselves worthy of everlasting life. The enabling power of redeeming grace rescues our soul from the effects of the fall of Adam and our own fleshly susceptibilities. Through the bounteous mercy and love of Jesus Christ, we are raised in immortality, we are forgiven of sin, we are given strength to do good works, and we are able to lay hold on eternal life and exaltation. We can be cleansed and healed by the grace and infinite atoning sacrifice of Jesus. His atonement, in an intimate way, was for each of us. To access the power of his atonement, we must do as Paul exhorted, "Examine yourselves, whether ye be in the faith; prove your own selves" (2 Corinthians 13:5).

AUGUST 7

Let the righteous smite me; it shall be a kindness:
and let him reprove me; it shall be an excellent oil.

PSALM 141:5

In looking back on our lives, it may surprise us to discover that some of our most meaningful lessons were learned from those who sought earnestly to correct us, to reprove us, to chastise us. No one enjoys reproof; we would prefer to be right all of the time and not require adjustment. No one enjoys having flaws or human frailties highlighted; we would prefer to assume that all is well in our souls. And no one delights in being told that attitudes or actions are in some way out of line; we would prefer to travel the road of life without course correction. But thank heaven for people who care enough about us to speak out, to risk offense, to assist us to become all we were intended to be. Such persons follow a divine example: "Verily, thus saith the Lord unto you whom I love, and whom I love I also chasten" (D&C 95:1; compare Hebrews 12:5–12).

AUGUST 8

Let every thing that hath breath
praise the Lord. Praise ye the Lord.
PSALM 150:6

While our worship and adoration of the God of heaven ought always to be couched in dignity and undertaken with a proper decorum, we would do well to think more often about how to express gratitude for unspeakable blessings. "I think the Lord's people should rejoice in him and shout praises to his holy name," Elder Bruce R. McConkie declared. "Cries of hosannah should ascend from our lips continually. When I think of the revealed knowledge we have about him whom it is life eternal to know, and the great plan of salvation which he has ordained for us . . . my soul wells up with eternal gratitude and I desire to raise my voice with the choirs above in ceaseless praise to him who dwells on high" (Conference Report, October 1973, 57). Such recognition, such acknowledgment, such deference lead us frequently to our knees in reverent humility and assist us to retain a remission of sins from day to day (Mosiah 4:11–12).

AUGUST 9

Trust in the Lord with all thine heart;
and lean not unto thine own understanding. In all thy
ways acknowledge him, and he shall direct thy paths.
PROVERBS 3:5–6

In a world of distrust and despair, there is one sure and steady source of sweet reassurance: the Lord. He can be trusted perfectly, without reservation. No matter how serious the trial, how deep the distress, he will never desert us, if we sincerely seek him. During our mortal sojourn we will be tested thoroughly until the Lord is certain we can be trusted in all things, regardless of the sacrifice involved. We are to look to the Lord, not to the world; trust him, not the wisdom of the foolish; follow his great plan of happiness, not the alluring temptations of the flesh. Our faith and gratitude are in the Lord. He loves each of us, but he trusts some more than others. How blessed to be both loved and trusted by the Lord! May the Lord say of us, "He may be trusted because of the integrity of his heart; and for the love which he has to my testimony I, the Lord, love him" (D&C 124:20).

AUGUST 10

Hear, ye children, the instruction of a father.

PROVERBS 4:1

Fathers have "the basic and inescapable responsibility to stand as the head of the family," said President Gordon B. Hinckley. "That does not carry with it any implication of dictatorship or unrighteous dominion. It carries with it a mandate that fathers provide for the needs of their families. Those needs are more than food, clothing, and shelter. Those needs include righteous direction and the teaching, by example as well as precept, of basic principles of honesty, integrity, service, respect for the rights of others, and an understanding that we are accountable for that which we do in this life, not only to one another but also to the God of heaven, who is our Eternal Father" (*Ensign*, November 1993, 60). The quality of a father's heart makes the difference for fathers and children: it is not in preaching but in serving, not in dictating but in building relationships in trust and tenderness. Fatherhood is of preeminent importance, here and hereafter.

AUGUST 11

Wisdom is the principal thing; therefore get wisdom: and with all thy getting get understanding.

PROVERBS 4:7

We are on this earth to get wisdom and understanding. Wisdom takes work, practice, and experience. To know when to be generous and when to hold back—that is wisdom. To know when to act and when to wait—that is wisdom. "Even a fool, when he holdeth his peace, is counted wise: and he that shutteth his lips is esteemed a man of understanding" (Proverbs 17:28). We have abundant opportunities to gain wisdom and understanding as we fail and stumble, as we learn and grow, as we interact with others, and as we are taught by the Spirit and educate our hearts. Whatever is at the center of our life will be the source of our wisdom and understanding. We are here to learn to put first things first, to develop charity and long-suffering, to become more like God.

Keep thy heart with all diligence; for out of it are the issues of life.
PROVERBS 4:23

Everything in life flows from the quality of our heart. We manifest integrity of heart as we strive to be "honest, true, chaste, benevolent, [and] virtuous" (Articles of Faith 1:13). Those with honest hearts, who do their best to develop the attributes of godliness, reap the rewards of a cheerful countenance and peace of mind. "Reformation of the world begins with reformation of self," said President Gordon B. Hinckley. "The example of our living will carry a greater influence than will all the preaching in which we might indulge. We cannot expect to lift others unless we stand on higher ground ourselves" (*Ensign,* September 2004, 4). For some life is relatively easy; for others it is a never-ending struggle. Sometimes the righteous are severely buffeted, and the wicked prosper for a season. But those who find lasting peace and joy are those whose hearts are firmly riveted on the Lord and his kingdom.

AUGUST 13

Ponder the path of thy feet.
PROVERBS 4:26

It often feels as if life is speeding up and time is flying. Life certainly seems more hectic and noisy than it once did. But with all the demands and busyness of life, we must take time to reflect, to ponder and consider where we're headed. President Gordon B. Hinckley said: "In my quiet moments, I think of the future with all of its wonderful possibilities and with all of its terrible temptations. I wonder what will happen to you in the next 10 years. Where will you be? What will you be doing? That will depend on the choices you make, some of which may seem unimportant at the time but which will have tremendous consequences" (*Ensign,* May 2004, 112). The direction we're headed is more important than the speed. To enjoy peace here and everlasting joy hereafter, we must stay faithfully on the gospel path and daily choose the Lord and his kingdom.

AUGUST 14

He that walketh uprightly walketh surely:
but he that perverteth his ways shall be known.
PROVERBS 10:9

The Proverbs contain wise sayings and insights. Often, the second part of each saying is the antithesis of the first. For example, "the integrity of the upright shall guide them: but the perverseness of transgressors shall destroy them" (Proverbs 11:3). Or, "better is the poor that walketh in his uprightness, than he that is perverse in his ways, though he be rich" (Proverbs 28:6). More important than textual analysis is the message of truth conveyed in these simple aphorisms. Wise men and women will be righteous people of faith and truth. They walk with confidence and security in the Lord because of their integrity and spirituality. Although not perfect, they live with inside-out congruence as they seek to emulate the Savior. Fools, on the other hand, will eventually be exposed as they teeter on the edge of wrongdoing and likely end up among the wicked. Those on the Lord's side walk uprightly with integrity.

AUGUST 15

The labour of the righteous tendeth to life.
PROVERBS 10:16

Work is necessary for our spiritual and physical wellbeing. Nothing happens without it—neither food nor crops nor spiritual or intellectual growth. Laziness is the enemy of righteousness, and slothfulness is a sin. "Thou shalt not be idle; for he that is idle shall not eat the bread nor wear the garments of the laborer" (D&C 42:42). Many of us would rather loaf than work, play than put our shoulder to the wheel, enjoy the fruits without putting forth the effort. But work enlarges the soul and strengthens the muscles—spiritual and physical. Work brings families together, creates character, and teaches responsibility. Work builds the kingdom and blesses countless people—at home and abroad. Those who work at something worthwhile, something meaningful, are the happiest people around. We can all find greater happiness by forgetting about ourselves, rolling up our sleeves, and going to work.

AUGUST 16

He that spareth his rod hateth his son:
but he that loveth him chasteneth him betimes.
PROVERBS 13:24

President Gordon B. Hinckley said: "I have never accepted the principle of 'spare the rod and spoil the child.' . . . Children don't need beating. They need love and encouragement" (*Ensign,* November 1994, 53). Good parents are like good shepherds who guide their sheep by gathering the lambs in their arms and gently leading them along (Isaiah 40:11). The shepherd's rod is never used for beating sheep; rather, it is used to protect the sheep and guard them from going in the wrong direction. The word translated "rod" in Proverbs 13:24 is translated in other places as "the word of God" (e.g., Micah 6:9; Isaiah 11:4). David, himself once a shepherd, said of the Lord, "Thy rod and thy staff they comfort me" (Psalm 23:4). A better translation of Proverbs 13:24 might be "he who withholds the word of God, hateth his son: he who loveth his son, corrects [or teaches] him early on [when he is young]."

AUGUST 17

A soft answer turneth away
wrath: but grievous words stir up anger.
Proverbs 15:1

Who among us has not felt the sting of anger, the bitterness of scorn? And we have all felt the warmth of kindness, the tender touch of gentleness. We each choose how to answer, how to act, how to respond. Elder Neal A. Maxwell counseled: "We can respond to irritation with a smile instead of scowl, or by giving warm praise instead of icy indifference. By our being understanding instead of abrupt, others, in turn, may decide to hold on a little longer rather than to give way. Love, patience, and meekness can be just as contagious as rudeness and crudeness" (*Ensign,* November 2000, 36). When we love, even in the presence of bitterness and anger, we create ever-widening circles of kindness and compassion. Peace comes to us when we return good for evil, when we are considerate in the presence of cruelty, when we are gentle in the presence of harshness.

AUGUST 18

A man's heart deviseth his way:
but the Lord directeth his steps.
PROVERBS 16:9

Each person born into this life has been given an invaluable gift—the Light of Christ. This light is an inner moral monitor, a discerning guide, the means by which we know right from wrong, good from evil, the relevant from the irrelevant. Those who attend to and follow this light are led to a higher light, even the light of the covenant gospel, whether in this life or the next. The Light of Christ is a precious commodity, but for those seeking to know the Lord and walk in his ways, it is insufficient; we also need the directing influence of the Holy Ghost. It is often the case that the Light of Christ will teach us correct principles and point us in the general direction we should pursue. The Holy Ghost will reveal to us specific practices and thus allow the Lord to direct our steps.

AUGUST 19

A merry heart doeth good like
a medicine: but a broken spirit drieth the bones.
PROVERBS 17:22

Life is to be enjoyed, not just endured. The happiest people are those who take pleasure in the glorious gospel, in the abundance of the Lord's blessings, in the exhilaration of simple moments and lighthearted joys. Even in anguish and sorrow, we can find moments of fun and laughter, of enjoyable mirth and pleasurable delight. Even in trials and tribulations, we can look on the bright side of things and accentuate the positive. Life is hard enough without living behind a woeful countenance of negativism. A merry heart is a grateful heart that rejoices in another day of life, for another opportunity to love and interact with God's creations. A merry heart is a humble heart that sees beauty even when it is surrounded by ugliness. A merry heart is a charitable heart that reaches out in love and kindness to others. We must do the best we can each day to live with a "glad heart and a cheerful countenance" (D&C 59:15).

AUGUST 20

The just man walketh in his integrity: his children are blessed after him.

PROVERBS 20:7

Integrity means to walk without hypocrisy or guile, to live truthfully, to be honest and trustworthy, to be whole. Integrity cannot be inherited or bought. No one can give it to us. We must earn and learn it in this mortal probationary school—and the process is a long one. Integrity is a trait that has to be tested in order to be perceived, because the world is full of people who claim to have integrity but their actions say otherwise. We find out the strength of our integrity by resisting the fiery darts of the adversary and standing steadfastly on the Lord's side of the line. Whatever our character, our integrity of heart, we create it day in and day out by the choices we make, the thoughts we think, the actions we take. But that is why we're here—to develop the attributes of godliness, to bring into our lives a full measure of the keystone virtue of integrity.

AUGUST 21

Train up a child in the way he should go:
and when he is old, he will not depart from it.
PROVERBS 22:6

Among the greatest sorrows of life is a child who strays from the path of righteousness and rejects the truths parents hold dear. Although there are no guarantees in parenting, there is always hope, a reason to hold on, to hope on, to go forward with faith—we simply cannot give up. When a child wanders, we fret and ache and sometimes despair, but we have sweet reassurances. Parents who have tried with all their hearts to rear children in love and righteousness, who have entered into sacred and binding familial covenants with the Lord, have the promise that their wayward children will be given opportunity to repent and return to the household of faith. Yes, as parents we must train and teach. But we must first and foremost build relationships of love and trust, embrace with an open and caring countenance, and live with an absence of self-righteousness and hypocrisy. Children need the abiding love of compassionate loved ones.

AUGUST 22

The borrower is servant to the lender.

PROVERBS 22:7

Debt is bondage; it is to be a slave to someone and something else. In a day when credit is easily available and countless people struggle daily under the pressures of crippling debt, spending a little less than we earn is not only good advice but a road map to happiness. The greatest riches of life are not found in material goods. Life's joys are found in the time we spend with friends and loved ones, in the peace of mind that comes from living modestly. Also, there is a sense of security and serenity that comes to those who structure their standard of living to build a little surplus. By living within our means and ignoring the siren song of acquisitiveness, we do not have to live under the constant burden of debt that can affect our marriages, our friendships, even our health. Indeed, the more we know about God's plan for the happiness of his children, the less of the world we need.

AUGUST 23

For as he thinketh in his heart, so is he.

PROVERBS 23:7

Our thoughts are a sure indication of the quality of our heart, which largely determines our happiness in life. The Lord said, "For where your treasure is, there will your heart be also" (Matthew 6:21). The treasure of our heart can make beauty out of ashes, sweet assurance out of heartache, and joy out of sorrow. At times, it would be easy to give in to cynicism and a bleak outlook. In reality, however, though physical comfort might be taken from us or worldly possessions lost, no one can rob us of good cheer. Our happiness is not stolen; it is given away, surrendered to situations that seem to demand that we yield our contentment and stop being happy. How valuable the knowledge that regardless of the challenges of mortality, we are loved by a God whose confidence in us never ceases. Happiness and thanksgiving are hard to dislodge from the heart of a person who knows that he is truly a child of God.

AUGUST 24

Apply thine heart unto instruction,
and thine ears to the words of knowledge.
PROVERBS 23:12

We take with us to the next life only what is in our heart and mind. The Prophet Joseph taught: "Whatever principle of intelligence we attain unto in this life, it will rise with us in the resurrection. And if a person gains more knowledge and intelligence in this life through his diligence and obedience than another, he will have so much the advantage in the world to come" (D&C 130:18–19). We can enlarge the heart and mind by studying, learning, and applying ourselves to instruction. We are here to gain light and knowledge, wisdom and truth. But in learning, we must spend time on that which is of inestimable value. The Lord said, "Seek ye diligently and teach one another words of wisdom; yea, seek ye out of the best books words of wisdom; seek learning, even by study and also by faith" (D&C 88:118). Some knowledge and truth matters more than others. The everlasting things are of greatest worth.

AUGUST 25

In multitude of counsellors there is safety.
PROVERBS 24:6

Millennia of experience teach us that there is wisdom in counsel, in surrounding oneself with others who are committed to the truth and eager to do what is right. In recent years, local leaders have been encouraged by the general leadership of the Church to expend more effort and take more seriously the privilege of counseling with our councils. A wise bishop, for example, is not necessarily one who has all of the answers, who knows how to act and what to say in every circumstance. Rather, a wise bishop is one who draws upon the combined strength, experience, and good judgment of his counselors, the auxiliary heads, and, in nonconfidential matters, his wife. Jesus himself explained that "where two or three are gathered together in my name, there am I in the midst of them" (Matthew 18:20). We invite the Spirit of the Lord when we invite the participation of wise counselors.

AUGUST 26

He that hath no rule over his own spirit is
like a city that is broken down, and without walls.
PROVERBS 25:28

We are continually surrounded by good and evil in a world of alluring choices. Enticing voices call out to us to seek pleasure, to look for the shortcut and easy way, to live for today and the carnal, sensual gratifications of the flesh (Mosiah 16:3). "The door to permissiveness, the door to lewdness and vulgarity and obscenity swings only one way," taught Elder Jeffrey R. Holland. "It only opens farther and farther; it never seems to swing back. Individuals can choose to close it, but it is certain, historically speaking, that public appetite and public policy will not close it. No, in the moral realm the only real control you have is self-control" (*Ensign,* November 2000, 39). As Jacob so powerfully stated, "Remember, to be carnally-minded is death, and to be spiritually-minded is life eternal" (2 Nephi 9:39). Self-mastery and righteous choices are the keys that unlock the door to abiding joy and everlasting peace.

AUGUST 27

Let another man praise thee, and not thine own mouth; a stranger, and not thine own lips.
PROVERBS 27:2

Because we are human, we desire to do things the right way and to have our actions acknowledged and approved by others. Our sense of worth often depends upon what other people think and how they praise or critique our actions. While such are perfectly normal reactions, they do not represent the state of mind toward which the Saints of the Most High should aspire. As time passes and as we grow in experience and mature in things of the Spirit, we begin to do the right things for the right reason. Jesus made a subtle comment that has haunting implications. He said simply, "I receive not honour from men" (John 5:41; compare John 8:54). That line speaks volumes. To have an eye single to the glory of God is to do the Lord's work and to do so seeking only the approval of the Person who guides this work and whose work this is.

AUGUST 28

He that covereth his sins shall not prosper: but whoso confesseth and forsaketh them shall have mercy.

PROVERBS 28:13

Speaking to those who hold the priesthood, the Lord said, "When we undertake to cover our sins, or to gratify our pride, . . . the heavens withdraw themselves [and] the Spirit of the Lord is grieved" (D&C 121:37). This universal principle applies to all people in all times. The Spirit of the Lord is grieved when we hide our sins with pride and hypocrisy. A sinful person may fool many people much of the time, and such a person may even seem to prosper for a season. But the Lord certainly knows the truth and cannot be fooled. In the end, sins will come back to haunt and torment the unrepentant. Those who are humble, who meekly approach the Lord for succor and rest, appreciate the power of repentance—forsaking sin and confessing it to the Lord and his authorized servants, if needed. Repentance is not to be dreaded and avoided but cherished as the way to find peace and everlasting joy.

AUGUST 29

Where there is no vision, the people perish: but he that keepeth the law, happy is he.
PROVERBS 29:18

In all gospel dispensations, the Church has been led by visionary prophets who see the big picture and inspire the Saints with a compelling vision of the future. We, too, can live with faith in the Lord and hope in the glorious gospel plan. We need more than a positive mental attitude, more than goals and dreams and personal mission statements. Those things may make a meaningful difference in our lives, but the Lord wants his followers to be people of faith, people who are obedient and worthy to receive personal revelation, people who draw upon the powers of heaven in humility, people whose confidence waxes strong in the presence of God (D&C 121:45). Vision and faith go hand in hand. When we have the meekness to look to him and live, we are blessed with a belief in others and in life, we recognize humanity's potential for greatness, and we see beyond the here and now. Every worthwhile effort is fueled by faith in the Lord.

AUGUST 30

Favour is deceitful, and beauty is vain:
but a woman that feareth the Lord, she shall be praised.
PROVERBS 31:30

Popularity and beauty come and go; the fleeting fashions of the day give way to those things that stand the test of time. Immutable and everlasting is the influence of a faithful and devoted woman. More often than not, it is her imprint that shapes the soul and educates the heart. "To help another human being reach one's celestial potential is part of the divine mission of woman," said Elder Russell M. Nelson. "As mother, teacher, or nurturing saint, she molds living clay to the shape of her hopes. In partnership with God, her divine mission is to help spirits live and souls be lifted. This is the measure of her creation. It is ennobling, edifying and exalting" (*Ensign,* November 1989, 22). A woman's essential nature is to nurture and love and counsel with kindness. Thanks be to God for loving and dedicated women who fear the Lord.

AUGUST 31

Vanity of vanities, sayeth the Preacher, vanity of vanities; all is vanity. What profit hath a man of all his labour which he taketh under the sun?

ECCLESIASTES 1:2–3

It is not difficult to come away from a reading of Ecclesiastes with a rather dismal and depressing perspective on life. It almost sounds as if the Preacher is one grand cynic, a person whose best efforts have been foiled and who has chosen to hate life and find little purpose in it all. The truth is, however, that Ecclesiastes contains a profound and meaningful message—a call for us to focus on things that matter most, to attend to matters eternal. We are counseled to put our trust in eternal verities, in lasting principles, in noble endeavors, and not to become preoccupied with the fleeting fads and telestial trends that so often bid for our attention. Indeed, the things of this world are vain: They are empty, without substance, and will pass away, having little effect on our final reward. Ecclesiastes is a somber call to prioritize our lives.

SEPTEMBER

Who knoweth whether thou art come to the kingdom for such a time as this?

ESTHER 4:14

SEPTEMBER 1

To every thing there is a season,
and a time to every purpose under the heaven.
ECCLESIASTES 3:1

We are in a rush. Many of us live on fast-forward without a pause button. We're obsessed with time—saving it, watching it, lamenting how fast it goes. In the process, we may forget that some things matter more than others. And in the end, we may lose more than we've gained by rushing through our days and forgetting the important things in life. We may also forget that each time of life presents its own pleasures and pressures. Don't wish for any part of life to be past. Age has its problems—and so does youth. We live through each season of life only once. Each one goes so quickly, and before we know it, it's gone. Enjoy this moment, today. There is a reason we are in this place at this time, and there is always potential and opportunity in the present moment. Despite all the demands and problems, all the worry and heartache, life is basically good. We should enjoy the journey.

SEPTEMBER 2

God shall judge the righteous and the wicked: for there is a time there for every purpose and for every work.
ECCLESIASTES 3:17

Every person born into mortality will be brought to a final judgment. There we will be judged according to the degree of knowledge and opportunity available during life, our works, and the desires of our heart. "The Final Judgment is not just an evaluation of the sum total of good and evil acts—what we have done," taught Elder Dallin H. Oaks. "It is an acknowledgment of the final effect of our acts and thoughts—what we have become. It is not enough for anyone just to go through the motions. The commandments, ordinances, and covenants of the gospel are not a list of deposits required to be made in some heavenly account. The gospel of Jesus Christ is a plan that shows us how to become what our Heavenly Father desires us to become" (*Ensign,* November 2000, 32). The final judgment rests with Christ. With justice and love and mercy, he will judge us on who we are and what we have become.

SEPTEMBER 3

Then shall the dust return to the earth as it was: and the spirit shall return unto God who gave it.
Ecclesiastes 12:7

As the years pass, we begin to realize that we are moving closer and closer to our death and that eventually our physical bodies will be placed in the grave, there to await the day of resurrection. But our spirit does not die, for in truth there is no death and there are no dead; there is only life. At the moment we breathe our last breath, our spirit makes a transition into the postmortal spirit world, there to be taught, trained, developed, refined, and readied for the time when spirit and body will be inseparably united in glorious immortality. We do not go directly into the immediate presence of our Lord at the time of death but rather go into a world where the Spirit of God is felt and the people of God are busily engaged in the work of the kingdom with an even greater tenacity than they were on this side of the veil.

SEPTEMBER 4

Fear God, and keep his commandments:
for this is the whole duty of man.
ECCLESIASTES 12:13

We show our reverence for God by keeping his commandments. As we willingly turn our hearts to heaven, we seek to bless others all over the world. Elder M. Russell Ballard has said, "Our duty lies in assisting others, through the power of the Spirit, to know and understand the doctrines and principles of the gospel. Everyone must come to feel that the doctrines of the Restoration are true and of great value. And everyone who accepts the message must strive to live the gospel by making and keeping sacred covenants and by participating in all of the ordinances of salvation and exaltation" (*Ensign,* November 2000, 75). When we enter into a covenant relationship with the Savior, we have a sacred obligation to spread the message of eternal life, the good news of the gospel. We reverence God by living his gospel, following his plan of happiness by precept and example, and helping others to do the same.

SEPTEMBER 5

For God shall bring every work into judgment, with every secret thing, whether it be good, or whether it be evil.
ECCLESIASTES 12:14

Resurrection and judgment are two sides of the same coin, for we come forth in the resurrection with a body suited and acclimated to a glory associated with the kingdom where we will dwell forever. We will not be surprised on the day of judgment, for our resurrected bodies will manifest the degree of glory we will receive. The scriptures repeatedly affirm that we will be judged according to our works. That does not mean that we will be judged according to the *merits* of our works, however, for the prophets repeatedly declare that eternal life comes to those who have learned to rely upon the "merits, and mercy, and grace of the Holy Messiah" (2 Nephi 2:8; compare Alma 22:14). Our good works, though necessary, are not sufficient. Our works manifest to God and man what we have become through the transforming power of the blood of Christ.

SEPTEMBER 6

Who is she that looketh forth as the morning, fair as the moon, clear as the sun, and terrible as an army with banners?
SONG OF SOLOMON 6:10

The Lord declared that he had begun the marvelous work and a wonder, "the beginning of the rising up and the coming forth of my church out of the wilderness—clear as the moon, and fair as the sun, and terrible as an army with banners" (D&C 5:14). The message of the restored gospel is clear. It is fair, or beautiful. To the ungodly and those who spurn righteousness, it is abhorrent. In referring to the growth of his Church in the last days, our Savior called upon us to "let my army become very great, and let it be sanctified before me, that it may become fair as the sun, and clear as the moon, and that her banners may be terrible unto all nations; that the kingdoms of this world may be constrained to acknowledge that the kingdom of Zion is in very deed the kingdom of our God and his Christ; therefore, let us become subject unto her laws" (D&C 105:31–32).

SEPTEMBER 7

The ox knoweth his owner,
and the ass his master's crib: but Israel doth not know,
my people doth not consider.
ISAIAH 1:3

God's accusation against Israel is a sobering one, an indictment that strikes at the very heart of what it means to be a chosen people, a people of covenant: Israel does not know her God. The Hebrew word translated In Isaiah 1:3 as "know" is *yadah,* which refers to a special, close knowledge. It is, in fact, the same word used in Genesis when we read that "Adam knew Eve his wife; and she conceived, and bare Cain" (Genesis 4:1). Jehovah's concern with Israel is that the kind of closeness, the kind of covenant intimacy that ought to exist between the God of heaven and his foreordained flock, simply does not exist. It is not sufficient for Israel to know *about* God, although that is a necessary beginning; Israel must seek for and live for the cleansing and guiding powers of the Spirit in order to gain "the mind of Christ" (1 Corinthians 2:16).

Hear the word of the Lord, ye rulers of Sodom; give ear unto the law of our God, ye people of Gomorrah. To what purpose is the multitude of your sacrifices unto me? saith the Lord: I am full of the burnt offerings of rams, and the fat of fed beasts.

ISAIAH 1:10–11

Adam and Eve were instructed to offer the firstlings of their flock as an offering unto God in similitude of the great and last sacrifice that would be offered in the meridian of time (Moses 5:5–8). Two and a half millennia later, God gave to a stumbling Israel the law of Moses, which included an intricate system of sacrifices and offerings. Within seven centuries and by the time of the prophet Isaiah, sacrificial offerings had begun to have little meaning to the people in general, and in many ways the means (the offerings as a type) had overshadowed the end (the Lord and his atoning sacrifice). God was not commanding Israel through Isaiah to cease offering animal sacrifices; rather, He was calling upon them to consider seriously why they were doing what they were doing. Truly, the law of Moses "is a shadow of those things which are to come . . . [and] that redemption cometh through Christ the Lord" (Mosiah 16:14–15).

SEPTEMBER 9

Come now, and let us reason together, saith the Lord:
though your sins be as scarlet, they shall be as white as snow;
though they be red like crimson, they shall be as wool.

ISAIAH 1:18

No more glorious message could be delivered than the message we know as the gospel of Jesus Christ—the good news, or glad tidings, that the Promised Messiah has come into the world and made real both the forgiveness of sins and the resurrection of the dead. Nothing could be more satisfying to the soul than the realization that we do not have to remain the way we are; we can change. But that change is not self-generated, something we do through our own grit and willpower, as important as personal discipline may be. Rather, and ironically, our filthy rags (Isaiah 64:6) are washed white through the cleansing blood of the Lamb of God. By the power of his blood, shed for us in Gethsemane and on the Cross, and through the medium of the Holy Ghost, our sins can be remitted, our souls liberated from the stain of misdeeds, and our burdens lightened. Praise God for the Atonement!

And it shall come to pass in the last days, that the mountain of the Lord's house shall be established in the top of the mountains . . . and all nations shall flow unto it.

ISAIAH 2:2

Who could have imagined that a small group of stalwart pioneers would tame a desert and create a city to which all nations would come? The centerpiece of that latter-day Zion is the temple. Isaiah prophesied, "And many people shall go and say, Come ye, and let us go up to the mountain of the Lord, to the house of the God of Jacob; and he will teach us of his ways, and we will walk in his paths: for out of Zion shall go forth the law, and the word of the Lord from Jerusalem" (Isaiah 2:3). The temple is a spiritual oasis, a sacred place of prayer and learning, a holy place to help us comprehend eternity. The temple gives us perspective that the world does not give; it is a link between earth life and eternity. Only through the eternal ordinances provided in temples can Heavenly Father's children return to his presence.

SEPTEMBER 11

Come ye, and let us walk in the light of the Lord.

ISAIAH 2:5

Surely, life has its storms. All of us, to one degree or another, are buffeted by the raging tempests around us. But we can have confidence in the Lord and his plan for our happiness. We depend on certain points of light as we navigate through life—beacons that shine through the darkness, steady and never faltering. We look to them for guidance: scriptures, words of the prophets, sweet whisperings of the Spirit, righteous loved ones, and inspired leaders. These beacons can help to "arouse the faculties of [our] souls" (Jacob 3:11) and lead us to the light of the Lord. As we strive to walk humbly and righteously before God, more light will come from heaven to enlighten our understanding and comfort our hearts. That light will become brighter even as the world darkens. Jesus Christ, the Light of the World, will lead his faithful followers to peace and joy in this life and everlasting life in the world to come.

Therefore thou [Jehovah] hast forsaken thy people the house of Jacob, because they be replenished from the east, . . . and they please themselves in the children of strangers.

ISAIAH 2:6

Surely there can be no more significant principle associated with the Atonement than the need, set forth in holy writ, to rely upon the Lord rather than upon ourselves or upon the arm of flesh (2 Nephi 4:34; 31:19; Moroni 6:4). One of the tragedies in the Old Testament, and a theme revisited far too often, was that Israel simply did not trust in the mighty arm of Jehovah to provide protection and comfort. Almost always, they looked to their own strength or sought to build confederations with surrounding nations rather than leaning upon the ample arm of the Lord of Hosts. Israel never seemed to learn the lesson that without God they could not succeed and that with his support and strength they could not fail.

SEPTEMBER 13

And the Lord will create upon every dwelling place of mount Zion, and upon her assemblies, a cloud and smoke by day, and the shining of a flaming fire by night: for upon all the glory shall be a defence.

ISAIAH 4:5

When Moses and the Israelites constructed the tabernacle, or tent of gathering, as their first temple, the divine *Shekinah* (holy cloud) frequently rested above the tabernacle as an indication that Jehovah was in his holy house. The prophecy in Isaiah 4:5 indicates that in the last days, when Zion has spread throughout the world, when the stakes of Zion have been established in all lands, and when temples of the Most High have begun to dot the earth, our Savior will once again dwell in wondrous ways and in a remarkable manner among the people of the covenant. His Spirit will be poured out miraculously, his glory will be manifest, and his people will have grown in spiritual grace to the point where they are prepared to welcome him into their own individual dwelling places.

SEPTEMBER 14

Woe unto them that call evil good, and good evil; that put darkness for light, and light for darkness; that put bitter for sweet, and sweet for bitter!

ISAIAH 5:20

Latter-day Saints have been counseled from the beginning to search and study the holy scriptures, to ponder and reflect upon the words of living apostles and prophets, and to seek the spirit of discernment in their everyday walk and talk. Such counsel is not intended only to make us a more intelligent people. In addition, regular immersion in the words of eternal life keep our souls attuned to the Infinite and our minds correlated with the counsel of heaven. As we cultivate the gift of the Holy Ghost, our desires will be educated, our judgment will be strengthened, and our consciences will be enhanced. We will not look to the world or to worldly people to determine our standards of right and wrong. Our ability to cling tenaciously to God's absolute truths will empower us to see through the shifting sands of secularity and the emptiness of moral relativism.

SEPTEMBER 15

And he will lift up an ensign to the nations from far, and will hiss unto them from the end of the earth: and, behold, they shall come with speed swiftly.

ISAIAH 5:26

We can only wonder what marvel Isaiah must have felt as he gazed upon the comings and goings of the people who would live in the last days. In Isaiah 5:26 he foresees the establishment of an "ensign to the nations," a clear allusion to the restoration of the everlasting gospel through the instrumentality of the Prophet Joseph Smith. That work of restoration would be an ensign, a banner, a standard, a rallying point to which people from throughout the earth would gather by exercising faith in the Lord Jesus Christ, repenting of their sins, receiving baptism and confirmation at the hands of legal administrators, and preparing themselves for the higher ordinances of the temple. The work would begin slowly, but with the passing of years, it would grow in magnitude such that "kings shall shut their mouths; for that which had not been told them shall they see; and that which they had not heard shall they consider" (3 Nephi 21:8).

SEPTEMBER 16

Then said I, Woe is me! for I am undone; because I am a man of unclean lips, . . . for mine eyes have seen the King, the Lord of hosts.

ISAIAH 6:5

Isaiah 6 represents what biblical scholars call a "throne theophany," a phenomenal experience in which an individual is caught up to the throne of God and shown his holiness and grandeur. Much as we would in such a setting, Isaiah felt unworthy to stand before holy beings. The King James word *undone* might also be rendered as *doomed, ruined,* or *lost.* Standing in the midst of pure holiness would undoubtedly cause the kind of introspective analysis that would result in such a reaction. Humans simply do not think like God, act like God, or speak like God, and Isaiah realized that only too well. As a part of his call to the ministry, Isaiah's preparation for the sacred work he was to do is symbolized by an angel placing a hot coal upon his mouth, thus allowing him to speak holy words and act in the name and by the authority of God.

SEPTEMBER 17

The Lord himself shall give you a sign; Behold, a virgin shall conceive, and bear a son, and shall call his name Immanuel.

ISAIAH 7:14

Seven hundred years before the birth of the Savior, Isaiah foresaw the glorious day when Immanuel, or "God with us," would make flesh his tabernacle. Nephi, one hundred years later, also foresaw the coming of the Son of God into mortality (1 Nephi 11:13–20). From the beginning of time, prophets and righteous seekers have looked to the meridian dispensation, when Christ would be born of Mary and come to earth to deliver all mankind. He would be born a babe in Bethlehem, learn from righteous Joseph and Mary, and "[increase] in wisdom and stature, and in favour with God and man" (Luke 2:52). As the only perfect person to walk the earth, he would willingly give his sinless life as a great and last sacrifice for all. As prophets foretold the birth of Jesus, they also saw the reasons for his mortal ministry—to offer an infinite atonement that would suffice for the sins of the world (Alma 34:10–14).

SEPTEMBER 18

For unto us a child is born, unto us a son is given: and the government shall be upon his shoulder: and his name shall be called Wonderful, Counsellor, The mighty God, The everlasting Father, The Prince of Peace.

ISAIAH 9:6

The magnificent messianic words of Isaiah echo down the centuries with the world's most important news: "For unto us a child is born" (Isaiah 9:6). The "us" spans the ages of time with exultant gratitude—the Son of God condescends to enter mortality, born as a babe in Bethlehem. Upon this perfect Child, this wonderful Counselor, this mighty God, rests the kingdom of God and all eternity. President Thomas S. Monson said, "[Jesus Christ] is a teacher of truth—but He is more than a teacher. He is the Exemplar of the perfect life—but He is more than an exemplar. He is the Great Physician—but He is more than a physician. He is the literal Savior of the world, the Son of God, the Prince of Peace, the Holy One of Israel, even the risen Lord" (*Ensign,* May 2004, 23). Our joy and thanksgiving know no bounds, our hope and sweet expectation know no end—all because Jesus was born.

There shall come forth a rod out of the stem of Jesse, and a Branch shall grow out of his roots. And in that day there shall be a root of Jesse, which shall stand for an ensign of the people; to it shall the Gentiles seek.

ISAIAH 11:1, 10

According to the Prophet Joseph Smith in March 1838, Jesus Christ is the stem of Jesse. Both the rod and the root appear to be references to the Prophet Joseph Smith. The rod is "a servant in the hands of Christ, who is partly a descendant of Jesse as well as of Ephraim, or of the house of Joseph, on whom there is laid much power." The root of Jesse is "a descendant of Jesse, as well as of Joseph, unto whom rightly belongs the priesthood, and the keys of the kingdom, for an ensign, and for the gathering of my people in the last days" (D&C 113:4, 6.) God certainly laid much power upon Joseph Smith, and he was one unto whom the priesthood rightly belonged (D&C 86:8–11). Brother Joseph and the work he set in motion were indeed the ensign to the nations and the means whereby God's people could be gathered in the last days.

The earth also is defiled under the inhabitants thereof; because they have transgressed the laws, changed the ordinance, broken the everlasting covenant.

ISAIAH 24:5

While it is true that noble men and women sought diligently through the generations to keep the flame of Christianity alive; that the Light of Christ and the influence of the Holy Ghost were felt by many who received answers to prayer and inspiration from heaven; and that great efforts were made to make the scriptures available to the people, yet apostolic authority and priesthood keys or directing power were lost to the earth following the deaths of the original apostles. Laws were transgressed. Ordinances such as the sacrament and baptism were changed dramatically. And the gospel in its fulness, which is the everlasting covenant, was broken when institutional priesthood power was taken from among the children of men. Not all was dark, and not all who lived during this period were wicked, for much that is decent and true within Christianity was preserved through the centuries. But a restoration was required.

SEPTEMBER 21

For thou hast been a strength to the poor, a strength to the needy in his distress, a refuge from the storm, a shadow from the heat.

ISAIAH 25:4

We live in a world of ever-increasing sinfulness and stress. The noise of confusion and distraction is all about us, beckoning with siren calls to one quick fix and then another. But there is no lasting peace, no real contentment outside the Lord and his infinite atonement. One of the glorious blessings of the Lord's loving sacrifice is that we can access the Savior's consoling and calming powers. Truly accepting the Lord and his atonement can heal us, reassure and refine us, and transform the vile and vicious, the wanton and worthless in life into something of supreme splendor and divine approbation. Indeed, it is in the healing balm of the Savior that "sorrow and sighing shall flee away" (Isaiah 35:10). With sincere searching and humble adoration, we find that the Savior is our strength in times of anguish and despair, our refuge in the inevitable storms of daily living, and our comforting shadow in the searing heat of life's heartaches.

SEPTEMBER 22

He will swallow up death in victory;
and the Lord God will wipe away tears from off all faces.
ISAIAH 25:8

To all those who mourn, the Lord will "give unto them beauty for ashes, the oil of joy for mourning, the garment of praise for the spirit of heaviness" (Isaiah 61:3). The Savior's death and resurrection offer us the promise of everlasting life; his unfathomable and infinite atonement gives us access to his grace and forgiveness; and his matchless power and pure love assure us that in our heartache we can find comfort and in our sorrow, peace. He said, "Come unto me, all ye that labour and are heavy laden, and I will give you rest. Take my yoke upon you, and learn of me; for I am meek and lowly in heart: and ye shall find rest unto your souls" (Matthew 11:28–29). If we come unto him with full purpose of heart, if we turn away from the world's enticements and seek to emulate his life (3 Nephi 27:27), we will know joy unspeakable and life unending.

SEPTEMBER 23

For the Lord hath poured out upon you the spirit of deep sleep, and hath closed your eyes: the prophets and your rulers, the seers hath he covered.

ISAIAH 29:10

Our God is gracious, not only in showering blessings and light and understanding upon his children but also in never delivering to his people more than they are prepared to receive. Such is merciful, for we are judged according to the light and knowledge we possess. During periods of apostasy, and even during periods when the gospel is on the earth, many are oblivious to the transcendent truths that are available and within easy reach. Many walk in darkness at noonday (D&C 95:6), because they are blind or have shielded themselves completely from light. When people close their minds, the prophets and seers eventually close their mouths.

And the vision of all is become unto you as the words of a book that is sealed, which men deliver to one that is learned, saying, Read this, I pray thee: and he saith, I cannot; for it is sealed.

ISAIAH 29:11

One sentiment that prevails during a period of apostasy is frustration—people want direction, but they do not know where to find it. The anxiety and frustration during a time when prophets and seers no longer speak is compared in Isaiah 29:11 to the frustration of having a book to read—presumably a book about significant matters—that cannot be opened. A similar analogy would be to hold in one's hands a book which is known to contain sacred and enlightening insights but which is inaccessible because it is locked. Only one who has received the key, even the key of knowledge, can open such a book. To the Prophet Joseph Smith were given "the keys of the mysteries, and the revelations which are sealed" (D&C 28:7) by God. To the Choice Seer were revealed "things which were from the foundation of the world, and the things which shall come from this time until the time of [the Lord's] coming" (D&C 35:18).

SEPTEMBER 25

This people draw near me with their mouth, and with their lips do honour me, but have removed their heart far from me.

ISAIAH 29:13

On many occasions, Jesus condemned hypocrites who "[draw] nigh unto me with their mouth, and [honour] me with their lips; but their heart is far from me" (Matthew 15:8). He also warned that those whose regard for the Lord is taught by the precepts of men are far from him in their hearts as well (Isaiah 29:13). Our understanding of God and our reverence of him come not through the traditions of men but through revelation from heaven and through gratitude for his bounteous goodness and mercy. Those with "integrity of . . . heart" (D&C 124:15) draw near unto the Lord with their lips *and* their hearts. They understand that the surest indication of our heart is how we think, talk, and act—what we do for others—which manifests our commitment to God and everlasting things. We are to turn our hearts to him with full purpose. We are to come unto Christ with integrity and remain, permanently and faithfully, until the end.

SEPTEMBER 26

Therefore, behold, I will proceed to do a marvellous work among this people, even a marvellous work and a wonder: for the wisdom of their wise men shall perish, and the understanding of their prudent men shall be hid.

ISAIAH 29:14

The marvelous work and a wonder of which Isaiah speaks began on a spring day in 1820 when the heavens opened anew and God spoke to man. From that day, the dispensation of the fulness of times, the keys and powers of the restoration of the gospel, and the saving truths in the Book of Mormon have gone forward out of obscurity to fill the earth with light. This marvelous work and wonder has confounded the skeptics and naysayers; it has baffled nonbelievers and perplexed the proud. It thrives because it is true, because it is the work of God. "Let the mountains shout for joy, and all ye valleys cry aloud; and all ye seas and dry lands tell the wonders of your Eternal King!" (D&C 128:23). The work is not yet finished, but the marvelous work and wonder of the restored gospel will continue to roll forth to bless countless people the world over and usher in the return of our Lord.

They also that erred in spirit shall come to understanding, and they that murmured shall learn doctrine.

ISAIAH 29:24

People who murmur, backbite, or continually complain are people who generally do not have the big picture—they do not see things as they are or as they really will be. Nephi wrote that "Laman and Lemuel, being the eldest, did murmur against their father. And they did murmur because they knew not the dealings of that God who had created them" (1 Nephi 2:12). We come to know the dealings of God as we search the scriptures, as we learn doctrine. "True doctrine, understood, changes attitudes and behavior," Elder Boyd K. Packer taught (Conference Report, October 1986, 20). When we understand the doctrine, the plan of salvation, we are in a position to make more accurate and productive decisions, to be a sustaining support rather than a meandering murmurer.

SEPTEMBER 28

Which say to the seers, See not; and to the prophets, Prophesy not unto us right things, speak unto us smooth things, prophesy deceits.

ISAIAH 30:10

Israel was scattered for rejecting the seers and the prophets of the Lord. Then, as now, the proud and disobedient could be described thus: "This is a rebellious people, lying children, children that will not hear the law of the Lord" (Isaiah 30:9). False prophets and preachers strive to lure us away from the path of righteousness. They want to "get you out of the way, turn aside out of the path, cause the Holy One of Israel to cease from before us" (Isaiah 30:11). How sad that some follow these foolish and blind guides and even become false prophets unto themselves. Some refuse to hear hard things from a prophet or have a seer witness their wickedness. Some want flattering permission for licentiousness or easy pronouncements that there is no sin. But true prophets are preachers of righteousness, teachers of truth. They jar the carnal mind with their testimonies, declare boldly the word of the Lord, and testify unflinchingly of our iniquities (Helaman 13:24–29).

SEPTEMBER 29

And the work of righteousness shall be peace; and the effect of righteousness quietness and assurance for ever.

ISAIAH 32:17

We live in a world of noise and confusion. With all the rattling that surrounds us, whence cometh peace? Not from a pep talk, a positive mental attitude, or a place in the country. Peace comes as we strive to focus our hearts more fully on Jesus and as we live in tune with the Spirit. Integrity of heart brings real peace and true joy. Meekness subdues our fleshly susceptibilities and turns our hearts to heaven. Obedience and submission to the Lord and his servants strengthen our resolve for righteousness and give us peace of mind. Peace descends upon those who focus on the Lord, who stay true to the truth, who take time to be holy. The apostle Paul said, "The peace of God, which passeth all understanding, shall keep your hearts and minds through Christ Jesus" (Philippians 4:7). Truly, enduring peace is found only in Christ.

SEPTEMBER 30

Who among us shall dwell with the devouring fire? who among us shall dwell with everlasting burnings? He that walketh righteously, . . . that stoppeth his ears from hearing of blood, and shutteth his eyes from seeing evil; he shall dwell on high.

ISAIAH 33:14–16

To dwell with devouring fire and everlasting burnings is to enjoy the sweet association of our Heavenly Father in the highest heaven. And who qualifies for such eternal association? Not only the person who walks and speaks righteously but also the one who refuses to become obsessed with the wickedness in his or her own day. To be sure, we must be vigilant; we must be spiritually on our toes, ever aware of Satan's machinations, always conscious of the evil throughout the world. In short, we must not be naïve. At the same time, however, we need not focus all of our attention, all of our conversation, on wickedness. There is much that is lovely and good and praiseworthy in this world, which we ought to acknowledge and think about continually (Philippians 4:8). The law of the harvest is at the heart of this matter: As we sow thoughts of righteousness, we shall reap the works of righteousness (Galatians 6:7–8).

October

Create in me a clean heart, O God;
and renew a right spirit within me.
Psalm 51:10

OCTOBER 1

The wilderness and the solitary place shall be glad for them; and the desert shall rejoice, and blossom as the rose.

ISAIAH 35:1

Isaiah foretold the day of restoration, when the desert shall blossom as the rose, the Lord will come, Israel will be gathered, and Zion shall prosper. The prophet also revealed the promise of millennial rejoicing: "It shall blossom abundantly, and rejoice even with joy and singing: the glory of Lebanon shall be given unto it, the excellency of Carmel and Sharon, they shall see the glory of the Lord, and the excellency of our God" (Isaiah 35:2). The earth will be renewed in that day, as the Lord said: "Therefore, will I not make solitary places to bud and to blossom, and to bring forth in abundance?" (D&C 117:7). Surely we have seen the desert blossom and blessings pour out upon Israel—but more, so much more, is yet to come. The land shall be fully renewed, believers will gather in increasing numbers to build up Zion, and all things will prepare and proclaim the day of the Lord.

OCTOBER 2

Strengthen ye the weak hands, and confirm the feeble knees. Say to them that are of a fearful heart, Be strong, fear not.

ISAIAH 35:3–4

Although mortality contains moments of happiness, we also walk through life with worries and problems, stresses and challenges. These trials and tribulations are our common lot. And because we are brothers and sisters in the family of God, we are all in this together. The interdependent nature of life means that we need each other in order to find real joy, to weather the storms that inevitably come our way, to lift and strengthen those who feel like giving up. Sometimes we need the kindness and strength of others, and sometimes we are the source of kindness and strength. Usually our kindness to others is not dramatic or extraordinary—it is manifested simply in the quality of our heart and the way we live, the way we extend ourselves, the way we treat others. A kind word and listening ear, gentle encouragement and support, the feeling that you trust and believe in another can make the biggest difference. Let us be strong in kindness.

OCTOBER 3

And an highway shall be there, and a way, and it shall be called The way of holiness; the unclean shall not pass over it.
ISAIAH 35:8

In a revelation given in November 1831 known as the appendix of the Doctrine and Covenants, we are told that in the very last days—at or just following the time of the Lord's second coming in glory—the ten northern tribes will be gathered into the fold of God. "And an highway shall be cast up in the midst of the great deep" (D&C 133:27). Such a scene evokes in the mind a miraculous event, some kind of road being created by God, over which the lost tribes will trek in their journey to Zion. Although stimulating, this scripture is highly symbolic. The ten tribes will gather as all others gather—namely, through conversion, by individuals joining the Church of Jesus Christ, by receiving the saving ordinances, and by congregating with the faithful. That is to say, they will traverse the highway of righteousness, the way of holiness, the gospel path that we have come to know as strait and narrow.

OCTOBER 4

In those days was Hezekiah sick unto death. . . . Then Hezekiah . . . said, Remember now, O Lord, I beseech thee, how I have walked before thee in truth, and with a perfect heart, and have done that which is good in thy sight.

ISAIAH 38:1–3

Hezekiah was a good man, one of the few righteous kings in Judah. He had kept the commandments of God. He had kept the faith. After having been informed by Isaiah that he was going to die, Hezekiah went before the Lord in pleading prayer and expressed a desire to be allowed to live longer. There is nothing unusual about such a request, for no doubt it happens every day throughout the earth. This was a prayer of faith—Hezekiah had lived the gospel, and he knew he had. He was a man possessed of deep spirituality, for there was within him a consciousness of victory over self, a quiet confidence by which he approached God in his plea that his life might be lengthened. Prayers of faith do not go unheard. Prayers of faith rend the heavens. Prayers of faith bring down the blessings of God. In this case, Hezekiah was granted a fifteen-year extension to his life.

OCTOBER 5

He shall feed his flock like a shepherd: he shall gather the lambs with his arm, and carry them in his bosom, and shall gently lead those that are with young.

ISAIAH 40:11

Jesus Christ is the Good Shepherd, and those who have come unto him by covenant are the sheep of his fold. The Good Shepherd knows his sheep, one by one, and knows how to lead, direct, counsel, and gather home each one because of his tender love for each one of his sheep. Because the sheep love him also, they know his voice, attend to his call, and respond to his invitation. The Good Shepherd loves his sheep enough that he willingly gave his own life for them. And his sheep know it.

OCTOBER 6

He giveth power to the faint; and to them that have no might he increaseth strength.

ISAIAH 40:29

There is much pain in this world today, much heartache and distress. Many of our Father's children have been worn down by the blows of adversity, battered by the vicissitudes of life, weakened by the roadblocks to peace that present themselves every day. Although a certain measure of tenacity on our part is necessary, and we must do our best to exercise grit and willpower in the face of oncoming opposition, in the long run our strength and our power must come from a source higher than ourselves. It is our Lord and Savior to whom we must turn in moments of weakness. It is the Holy One of Israel upon whom we must lean when we are tempted to be less than holy, and it is the Lord God Omnipotent to whom we reach when we feel faint and have not the strength to go on. Indeed, Christ is the answer to all of life's vexing questions, the solution to all our perplexing problems.

OCTOBER 7

They that wait upon the Lord shall renew their strength; they shall mount up with wings as eagles; they shall run, and not be weary; and they shall walk, and not faint.

ISAIAH 40:31

An eagle knows when a storm is coming long before it breaks. The eagle will fly to a high spot and wait for the winds to come. When the storm hits, the great bird sets its wings so that the wind will lift it above the storm. While the storm rages below, the eagle soars, actually using the storm to lift it higher. We, too, can feel God's peace even in the midst of a storm. We can become refined and strengthened, wiser and more teachable, by enduring well the challenges of life. When the storms of life come, as they surely will, we can rise above them by setting our hearts on everlasting things. We are lifted by beautiful music that stirs the soul; we are lifted by spending time in prayer and contemplation; we are lifted as we reach out to others in kindness; we are lifted as we turn our hearts to heaven and allow God's power to comfort our souls.

OCTOBER 8

Fear thou not; for I am with thee: be not dismayed; for I am thy God: I will strengthen thee; yea, I will help thee; yea, I will uphold thee with the right hand of my righteousness.

ISAIAH 41:10

President Gordon B. Hinckley, a man of great faith, said: "Who among us can say that he or she has not felt fear? . . . We suffer from the fear of ridicule, the fear of failure, the fear of loneliness, the fear of ignorance. Some fear the present, some the future. Some carry the burden of sin and would give almost anything to unshackle themselves from those burdens but fear to change their lives. Let us recognize that fear comes not of God, but rather that this gnawing, destructive element comes from the adversary of truth and righteousness. Fear is the antithesis of faith. It is corrosive in its effects, even deadly. . . . We need not fear as long as we have in our lives the power that comes from righteously living by the truth which is from God our Eternal Father. Nor need we fear as long as we have the power of faith" (*New Era,* January 2002, 6–7).

OCTOBER 9

To open the blind eyes, to bring out the prisoners from the prison, and them that sit in darkness out of the prison house.

ISAIAH 42:7

Joseph Smith spoke of the Savior's visit to the spirits in prison: "And what did He preach to them? That they were to stay there? Certainly not! . . . It is very evident from this [Luke 4:18; Isaiah 42:7] that He not only went to preach to them, but to deliver, or bring them out of the prison house" (*Teachings,* 219). Another passage in the book of Isaiah refers to Christ's freeing the bands of spiritual and physical death: "The Spirit of the Lord God is upon me; because the Lord hath anointed me to preach good tidings unto the meek; he hath sent me to bind up the brokenhearted, to proclaim liberty to the captives, and the opening of the prison to them that are bound" (Isaiah 61:1). On both sides of the veil, we rejoice as Christ throws wide the prison doors.

OCTOBER 10

I am the Lord: that is my name: and my glory will I not give to another, neither my praise to graven images.

ISAIAH 42:8

Graven images are false gods that lead to emptiness and despair. Idols are anything that denies, supplants, or takes away from the one true God of Israel. For some, false gods may be money and social status; for others, intellectualism and elitism; for others, worldly achievement and self-fulfillment. We all have our temptations and susceptibilities, and those things run the danger of becoming our god—the very thing that leads ultimately to hopelessness. Even the faithful can get off the true path slowly, imperceptively, spending a little too much time in the vain and empty things of the world. Before they know it, they're in a place very different from the one they imagined they would be in. False gods usually work insidiously, little by little. Pride is always at the root. The one true God has given us a plan of salvation, a way to everlasting peace and happiness. Let us not be deceived.

Fear not: for I am with thee: I will bring thy seed from the east, and gather thee from the west; I will say to the north, Give up; and to the south, Keep not back: bring my sons from far, and my daughters from the ends of the earth.

ISAIAH 43:5–6

Although we generally tend to think of the gathering as the movement of large groups of people to an appointed geographical spot, in fact the gathering begins as an individual response to the witness of the Spirit that Jesus is the Christ, that his gospel is the only means by which sin and death can be conquered, and that his gospel is incorporated into one's life through receiving its first principles and ordinances. In short, we gather first to Christ and his gospel and then to the lands of our inheritance or to the congregations of the faithful. People from the north and the south and the east and the west have gathered, and are being gathered, and will yet be gathered, as they respond affirmatively to the message of salvation preached by the messengers of salvation.

OCTOBER 12

I, even I, am the Lord; and beside me there is no saviour.

ISAIAH 43:11

Although it is true that Jehovah was responsible for the creation of worlds without number (Moses 1:33; 7:30), the scriptures do not speak of any Savior other than Jesus Christ. In fact, latter-day revelation attests that his atonement was infinite and eternal and that it reached well beyond the bounds of this earth. What he created, he redeems. Truly, as we sing in the hymn, "There was no other good enough to pay the price of sin" (*Hymns,* no. 194). We do not suppose that there was some substitute savior, some second-string redeemer, standing in the wings to assume center stage if Jesus of Nazareth had refused to drink the bitter cup and take up the awful burden of the Atonement. Just as the apostle Paul stated, "To us there is but one God, the Father" (1 Corinthians 8:6), so to us there is but one Savior, one Lord and Deliverer, one Hope of Israel.

OCTOBER 13

I am the first, and I am the last; and beside me there is no God.

ISAIAH 44:6

Nothing should come before God in our affection and obedience. Those who trust the true God of Israel will be strengthened in their convictions and buoyed up in their difficulties. "Fear ye not, neither be afraid: have not I told thee from that time, and have declared it? ye are even my witnesses. Is there a God beside me? yea, there is no God; I know not any" (Isaiah 44:8). By contrast, graven images and false gods are made by profiteers. The maker of a wooden idol benefits more from the wood he burns to warm himself and cook his food than from the wood he makes into a wooden god (Isaiah 44:9–20). Gods of wood, stone, or steel are all idols that cannot answer prayers, extend compassion, or offer salvation. Just as the fool says there is no God (Psalm 14:1), the fool also says this false idol is god. Let us "be still, and know that [God is] God" (Psalm 46:10).

OCTOBER 14

That saith of Cyrus, He is my shepherd, and shall perform all my pleasure: even saying to Jerusalem, Thou shalt be built; and to the temple, Thy foundation shall be laid.

ISAIAH 44:28

Isaiah 44:28 and 29 have been identified by modern biblical scholars as an example of a portion of Isaiah that was written either by a later Isaiah or by Isaiah's disciples. They reached that conclusion by observing that reference is here made to Cyrus, king of Persia, some two centuries before Cyrus was born. They suggest that this passage could not possibly have been spoken and written during the days of Isaiah the prophet (approximately 742–701 B.C.). Although the wisdom of man suggests that biblical study entails putting aside such simplistic notions as divine intervention, miracles, and predictive prophecy, believers respond by bearing testimony of God's ability to know the future and share that knowledge with his prophets and seers.

OCTOBER 15

I have made the earth, and created man upon it:
I, even my hands, have stretched out the heavens, and all
their host have I commanded.

ISAIAH 45:12

The premortal Jehovah, even Jesus Christ, created the heavens and earth and worlds without number (John 1:1–3; Colossians 1:16–17; D&C 76:22–24). "For thus saith the Lord that created the heavens; God himself that formed the earth and made it; he hath established it, he created it not in vain, he formed it to be inhabited: I am the Lord; and there is none else" (Isaiah 45:18). This creative work was done under the direction of the Father and by his power. The Father and Son are one—one in purpose, desire, mission, and work: "To bring to pass the immortality and eternal life of man" (Moses 1:39). We have been blessed with this glorious world and the great plan of happiness so that we can perform *our* mission and work: "Behold, this is your work, to keep my commandments, yea, with all your might, mind and strength" (D&C 11:20).

OCTOBER 16

But Israel shall be saved in the Lord with an everlasting salvation: ye shall not be ashamed nor confounded world without end.

ISAIAH 45:17

Our Heavenly Father's dealings with his chosen people through the centuries has been challenging at best. The descendants of Abraham, Isaac, and Jacob have not always lived in a manner befitting their calling. They have not always known their God and walked in his statutes. Nevertheless, the merciful Holy One of Israel refuses to give up on his people. As the allegory of Zenos dramatizes (Jacob 5), God simply will not let Israel go! He will continue to send his prophets, chasten them when needed, scatter and gather them to all parts of the earth, and labor tirelessly to create among them a kingdom of priests and priestess, kings and queens. In the end, in ways that now seem marvelous to our understanding, Israel will be saved (Romans 11:26).

OCTOBER 17

The word is gone out of my mouth in righteousness,
and shall not return, That unto me every knee shall bow,
every tongue shall swear.
ISAIAH 45:23

The day will surely come, and is not far distant, when the Lord will return in glory and we will choose either him or the world. As beautifully expressed by Elder Neal A. Maxwell, "We are free to choose the mortal perks with their short shelf life. However, ahead lies that great moment when every knee shall bow and every tongue confess that Jesus is the Christ! . . . Then the galleries and the mortal thrones will be empty. Even the great and spacious building will fall—and resoundingly! . . . Then, too, those who have lived without God in the world will confess that God is God! . . . Meanwhile, His character and attributes should evoke adoration and emulation from us" (*Ensign,* November 2000, 37). This life is the time to come unto Christ and be saved, to take his name upon us with full purpose of heart.

OCTOBER 18

And [the Lord] said, It is a light thing that thou shouldest be my servant to raise up the tribes of Jacob, and to restore the preserved of Israel: I will also give thee for a light to the Gentiles, that thou mayest be my salvation unto the end of the earth.

ISAIAH 49:6

Jehovah reminds his people that theirs is a broader responsibility than many Israelites supposed. To be a chosen people was a responsibility as well as a blessing, a responsibility associated with spreading the principles of the eternal gospel to all nations, kindreds, tongues, and peoples. Israel was to do more than to see to their own necessities; the message of salvation was to be taken to all the world, and Israel was commissioned to take it. When Jehovah said it was a "light thing" to raise up the tribes of Jacob, what he meant was that it was not enough for the twelve tribes to be a light to one another. Rather, they were to be a light unto the Gentiles, who are the nations of the earth. As the Lord explained through the Prophet Joseph Smith, "Therefore, blessed are ye if ye continue in my goodness, a light unto the Gentiles, and through this priesthood, a savior unto my people Israel" (D&C 86:11).

OCTOBER 19

Can a woman forget her sucking child, that she should not have compassion on the son of her womb? yea, they may forget, yet will I not forget thee. Behold, I have graven thee upon the palms of my hands.

ISAIAH 49:15–16

God's promise to gather and restore his scattered children receives repetitive emphasis in the Old Testament and the Book of Mormon. Although Israel had given her God every reason to forsake and forget her, to choose another people to represent him, the Almighty would forevermore be true to his word. He could not forget Israel any more than a woman could forget her child. For one thing, he had graven them on the palms of his hands. The tokens of the Crucifixion, the emblems of the infinite Atonement, were everlasting reminders to the Redeemer of what he had done and what he would do to preserve and protect his beloved.

OCTOBER 20

The children which thou shalt have, after thou hast lost the other, shall say again in thine ears, The place is too strait for me: give place to me that I may dwell.

ISAIAH 49:20

We rejoice in the growth that has taken place in The Church of Jesus Christ of Latter-day Saints since 6 April 1830. In fact, sometimes we become so excited about it that we forget we still are only a tiny fraction of the earth' s population. The gathering that has taken place since the organization of the Church has been steady and sure, but until now we have mostly been gathering the gatherers; that is, most of the people who have come into the Church are descendants of the patriarch Joseph. The great day of gathering is yet to be, a time foreseen by Nephi when the Saints of God would be upon all the face of the earth and in every land and culture (1 Nephi 14:12). This is the Lord's work, and he is at its head. The work will be accelerated, tens of millions will come into the fold, and the fruits of Mormonism will be felt in every land and among every people.

OCTOBER 21

Thus saith the Lord God, Behold, I will lift up mine hand to the Gentiles, and set up my standard to the people: and they shall bring thy sons in their arms, and thy daughters shall be carried upon their shoulders.

ISAIAH 49:22

Spiritually speaking, Nephi explained that the prophecy recorded in Isaiah 49:22 represents the people of Israel being invited to the gospel banquet in the last days and being treated like royalty. As he says, the Restoration would take place in "a mighty nation among the Gentiles" (1 Nephi 22:7), and a marvelous work and a wonder would entail the gospel going forth from cultural Gentiles (Joseph Smith and the Latter-day Saints) to latter-day descendants of Israel (the Lehites and the Jews). In a literal sense, the mighty nation among the Gentiles, the United States of America, has been and continues to be a great supporter of the descendants of Abraham. Prophecies concerning the prosperity of God's chosen people have been fulfilled, and all the prophecies will yet be fulfilled (1 Nephi 22:7–11).

OCTOBER 22

Thus saith the Lord, Where is the bill of your mother's divorcement, whom I have put away? or which of my creditors is it to whom I have sold you? Behold, for your iniquities have ye sold yourselves, and for your transgressions is your mother put away.

ISAIAH 50:1

Isaiah 50:1 is a sober reminder that when we sin and lose the Spirit of the Lord in our lives, it is we who have moved, not the Lord. The Bridegroom has not divorced his bride, although for seasons at a time she went whoring after other gods and proved unworthy of her chosen designation. Having sold herself through her iniquities, her only hope is to be bought back, to be purchased, or, as the scriptures testify, to be redeemed. Jesus Christ, the Promised Messiah, has offered to redeem her and re-esteem her as a holy nation. Through exercising faith in the Lord Jesus and demonstrating godly sorrow for her sins, Israel may be reinstated in the royal family.

OCTOBER 23

Awake, awake; put on thy strength, O Zion; put on thy beautiful garments, O Jerusalem. . . . Shake thyself from the dust; arise, and sit down, O Jerusalem: loose thyself from the bands of thy neck, O captive daughter of Zion.

ISAIAH 52:1–2

Isaiah calls upon the people of God to wake up to a realization of who they were, who they are, and what they may become. Israel was destined for greatness, and she must shake off her complacency and her mediocrity in order to assume her royalty. As the revelations declare, "to put on her strength is to put on the authority of the priesthood, which she, Zion, has a right to by lineage; also to return to that power which she had lost" (D&C 113:8). Israel will be loosed from her bands as she gathers into the true fold of God and begins once again to enjoy the revelations of heaven.

OCTOBER 24

How beautiful upon the mountains are the feet of him that bringeth good tidings, that publisheth peace; that bringeth good tidings of good, that publisheth salvation; that saith unto Zion, Thy God reigneth!

ISAIAH 52:7

In the Sermon on the Mount, the Master taught: "Blessed are the peacemakers; for they shall be called the children of God" (Matthew 5:9). The God of heaven is surely pleased with those who seek to establish peace among feuding nations, but this passage has a much broader meaning. Lasting peace can come to the earth only as the gospel of Jesus Christ is allowed to enter the minds and hearts of persons everywhere. The most glorious and blessed thing we can do is to teach and testify of the gospel, to lead others to the kind of spiritual rebirth that overcomes fear and enmity, to teach them to live as the Prince of Peace lived. That is why the Whitmer brothers were instructed that "the thing which will be of the most worth unto you will be to declare repentance unto this people, that you may bring souls unto me, that you may rest with them in the kingdom of my Father" (D&C 15:6; 16:6).

OCTOBER 25

Depart ye, depart ye, go ye out from thence, touch no unclean thing; go ye out of the midst of her; be ye clean, that bear the vessels of the Lord.

ISAIAH 52:11

The Lord repeatedly says, "Be ye clean, that bear the vessels of the Lord" (3 Nephi 20:41; D&C 38:42; 133:5). Elder Jeffrey R. Holland taught: "As priesthood bearers not only are we to *handle* sacred vessels and emblems of God's power—think of preparing, blessing, and passing the sacrament, for example—but we are also to *be* a sanctified instrument as well. Partly because of what we are to *do* but more importantly because of what we are to *be,* the prophets and apostles tell us to 'flee . . . youthful lusts' and 'call on the Lord out of a pure heart.' They tell us to be clean" (*Ensign,* November 2000, 39). We must pray for help; we must resist the pull of the world and live worthy of the Spirit; we must stand in holy places and be clean.

OCTOBER 26

For he [Jesus] shall grow up before him [the Father] as a tender plant, and as a root out of a dry ground: he hath no form nor comeliness; and when we shall see him, there is no beauty that we should desire him.

ISAIAH 53:2

Like all his mortal brothers and sisters, Jesus came to earth as a helpless infant, totally dependent upon the love and care of his parents. He grew up in a humble home, served under his earthly father to learn the skills of carpentry, and knew firsthand what it was to sweat and toil and feel fatigue. There can be no doubt that some things about the young Jesus made him distinctive—"he spake not as other men, neither could he be taught; for he needed not that any man should teach him" (JST Matthew 3:25)—yet he was not to be recognized as the Messiah because he was more handsome than the average Jewish boy or because his clothing in some way distinguished him. No, people would come to know that Jesus is the Christ by the quiet whisperings of the Holy Spirit. God the Son was to be known only by the power of the Spirit of God (1 Corinthians 2:11–14).

OCTOBER 27

Surely he hath borne our griefs, and carried our sorrows:
yet we did esteem him stricken, smitten of God, and afflicted.

ISAIAH 53:4

The prophecy of Isaiah was that the Messiah would be called Immanuel, a Hebrew word that means simply "God is with us." Indeed, when the Son of God came to earth he became human. In a very real sense, Jesus' whole life was an important part of the Atonement in his capacity to know rejection, feel pain, and experience the trials of the telestial world. All these things contributed to his ability to feel empathy for his brothers and sisters. In Gethsemane and on Golgotha Jesus was exposed to the "fierceness of the wrath of Almighty God" (D&C 76:107). There he suffered the effects of the sins, misdeeds, omissions, fears, temptations, sicknesses, and infirmities of all (Alma 7:11–12). In this way he bore our grief and carried our sorrows. Now we can speak of it reverently and mysteriously. Perhaps one day we shall understand how this magnificent miracle was brought to pass by the God who became man.

All we like sheep have gone astray; we have turned every one to his own way; and the Lord hath laid on him the iniquity of us all.

ISAIAH 53:6

Staying on the path of righteousness means that we shun selfishness and preoccupation with the allurements of the world, live worthy of the quiet whisperings of the Spirit, keep our eyes and hearts firmly riveted on the first principles of the gospel, and follow the Lord and his authorized servants in word and deed. President Thomas S. Monson said: "On the journey along the pathway of life, there are casualties. Some depart from the road markers which lead to life eternal, only to discover that the detour chosen ultimately leads to a dead end. Indifference, carelessness, selfishness, and sin all take their costly toll in human lives. There are those who, for unexplained reasons, march to the sound of a different drummer, later to learn they have followed the Pied Piper of sorrow and suffering" (*Ensign,* November 2000, 66). The one sure pathway to peace and everlasting joy is to follow the Good Shepherd.

OCTOBER 29

Yet it pleased the Lord to bruise him; he hath put him to grief.

ISAIAH 53:10

How could our Heavenly Father be pleased in any way with the horrendous suffering associated with the Garden and the Cross? Of course the Father was not pleased to see his Son in such bitter anguish; no parent could view such a scene and not desire to rush forward to snatch a child away from such incomprehensible suffering. Isaiah 53:10 teaches us that despite what it cost the Father to give his Son in sacrifice to the human race, the almighty Elohim was grateful that the long-prophesied atonement was finally an accomplished fact, something which disciples could now look back upon with gratitude and thanksgiving.

OCTOBER 30

When thou shalt make his soul
an offering for sin, he shall see his seed.
ISAIAH 53:10

Once Christ had made his expiatory offering and completed the Atonement, he gave up the ghost and passed into the postmortal world of spirits. There, in paradise, he was greeted by "his seed," an "innumerable company of the spirits of the just," those who had given heed to the words of the prophets through the ages (Mosiah 15:10–13; D&C 138:12). Is it not also possible that he who ministers "one by one" could have seen each of us and the myriads of other mortals pass before him in panoramic vision during his darkest hours? Is it possible that when he was tempted to turn away from the bitter cup he might have thought, "No, I must go through with this, for David or Sarah or Deborah will one day depend upon me"? We do not know the meaning of all things, but like Nephi, we know with a certainty that God loves his children (1 Nephi 11:17).

OCTOBER 31

And all thy children shall be taught of the Lord; and great shall be the peace of thy children.

ISAIAH 54:13

We have a sacred responsibility as parents to rear our children in love and righteousness, to take seriously our parental stewardship, to live worthy of emulation. President Gordon B. Hinckley said: "What a tragedy it is, what a bleak and terrible thing to witness a son or daughter on whom you counted so much walk the tortuous path that leads down to hell. On the other hand, what a glorious and beautiful thing it is to see the child of your dreams walk with head up, standing tall, unafraid, and with confidence, taking advantage of the tremendous opportunities that open around him or her. Isaiah said, 'All thy children shall be taught of the Lord; and great shall be the peace of thy children' (Isa. 54:13). So lead your sons and daughters, so guide and direct them from the time they are very small, so teach them in the ways of the Lord, that peace will be their companion throughout life" (*Ensign,* November 2000, 52).

NOVEMBER

Surely he hath borne our griefs, and carried our sorrows: yet we did esteem him stricken, smitten of God, and afflicted.

ISAIAH 53:4

NOVEMBER 1

Ho, every one that thirsteth, come ye to the waters,
and he that hath no money; come ye, buy, and eat; yea, come,
buy wine and milk without money and without price.
ISAIAH 55:1

Salvation, which is eternal life, which is exaltation, is the greatest of all the gifts of God (D&C 6:13; 14:17). It is not something that may be bartered for, purchased, or even earned. We do not earn a gift but rather receive it. Our good works represent our effort to demonstrate our love for God and thus the seriousness of our discipleship. There are not enough home teaching visits, loaves of bread given to neighbors, visits to the sick, thoughtful greetings, prayers, or church meetings to save us. Our salvation rests securely on the truth that God the Son did for us what we could never do for ourselves. He offers to us his unearned divine assistance, his unmerited divine favor, and his enabling power. Faith in the Lord Jesus Christ (and its attendant elements, repentance and baptism) opens the door to the receipt of his marvelous gift.

NOVEMBER 2

Wherefore do ye spend money for that which is not bread? and your labour for that which satisfieth not? hearken diligently unto me, and eat ye that which is good, and let your soul delight itself in fatness.

ISAIAH 55:2

One of the great lessons to learn in this life is where and how best to spend our time and expend our efforts. Millions upon millions of people rush about the earth seeking fulfillment, looking for lasting love in all the wrong places. It just may be that the gift of discernment can do much more than help us distinguish between right and wrong. It can also help us to perceive what things are worthy of our time and interest and what things (though seemingly good) are better left undone. We cannot do everything, nor can we possibly be engaged in every worthy endeavor. Nothing could be more tragic than to have spent our life laboring in secondary causes.

NOVEMBER 3

Incline your ear, and come unto me: hear, and your soul shall live; and I will make an everlasting covenant with you.

ISAIAH 55:3

All of us are pilgrims. Those with enduring faith in Christ make their way through life learning and growing, making mistakes and repenting, all the while striving to overcome the world. Sometimes we lose our way or lose sight of Whose we *really* are—sons and daughters of a loving Father in Heaven. President Thomas S. Monson said: "Come from your wandering way, weary traveler. Come to the gospel of Jesus Christ. Come to that heavenly haven called home. Here you will discover the truth. Here you will learn the reality of the Godhead, the comfort of the plan of salvation, the sanctity of the marriage covenant, the power of personal prayer. Come home" (*Ensign,* November 2000, 66). We are to "come unto [the Lord] with a broken heart and a contrite spirit" (3 Nephi 12:19), willing to do all that is necessary to live the gospel fully and keep the commandments. Come home, enter into covenants with Christ, and keep them.

NOVEMBER 4

For my thoughts are not your thoughts, neither are your ways my ways. . . . For as the heavens are higher than the earth, so are my ways higher than your ways, and my thoughts than your thoughts.

ISAIAH 55:8–9

The Lord is perfect. He knows all things and is flawless in all virtues and heavenly attributes. He is not a perpetual student ever learning or developing a fulness of knowledge, goodness, or wisdom. He is perfect. Jacob said, "Behold, great and marvelous are the works of the Lord. How unsearchable are the depths of the mysteries of him; and it is impossible that man should find out all his ways. And no man knoweth of his ways save it be revealed unto him; wherefore . . . despise not the revelations of God" (Jacob 4:8). We come to know the Lord by seeking the Spirit for our guide, so that we are not deceived (D&C 45:57). We know his ways by feasting upon the words of eternal life in the scriptures and from our living apostles and prophets. His ways are revealed through humble prayer and quiet pondering of the plan of happiness. We can have confidence in his perfect knowledge and everlasting mercy.

NOVEMBER 5

There is no peace, saith my God, to the wicked.

ISAIAH 57:21

In ancient times, the Israelites used a balm made from a bush that grew in Gilead. This fragrant balm was applied to wounds and was renowned for its healing power. For Israel, and for God-fearing people throughout the ages, the balm in Gilead has become a symbol of God's love and mercy. Tenderly applied, it promises healing and renewal. The balm of Gilead still offers solace and comfort. When life's twists and turns throw us off balance, we can steady ourselves by seeking God. When we feel angst about what the future holds and experience turmoil about our ability to carry on, we can trust God. The Psalmist declared: "Rest in the Lord, and wait patiently for him: fret not thyself. . . . The meek shall inherit the earth; and shall delight themselves in the abundance of peace" (Psalm 37:7, 11). Peace, healing, and joy come to those who turn away from the wickedness of the world and seek the Lord in righteousness.

NOVEMBER 6

Is not this the fast that I have chosen? To loose the bands of wickedness, to undo the heavy burdens, and to let the oppressed go free, and that ye break every yoke?

ISAIAH 58:6

There is power, consummate power, to be derived from earnest fasting and prayer. When we fast, as we deny the demands and appetites of our physical body, we begin to focus upon things spiritual and eternal, to hunger and thirst after righteousness. While fasting we find our hearts drawn out to the hungry and the needy. When we fast, we feel driven to our knees to plead for divine strength, forgiveness, and empowerment. When we fast, we become conscious of a quiet spiritual confidence, an awareness that we are masters of our bodies, victors over self. That is the essence of spirituality. Isaiah 58:6 is one of the few places in scripture where we learn the power of fasting and prayer in overcoming temptation, putting off the allurements of the flesh, and receiving a remission of sins. This is the fast that God has ordained for his children.

NOVEMBER 7

Is it not to deal thy bread to the hungry, and that thou bring the poor that are cast out to thy house?

ISAIAH 58:7

In the Lord's Church, fasting and prayer are to be accompanied by the payment of a generous fast offering. Through our fasting, we become more aware of those who struggle to make ends meet, of those who go to bed hungry each night. Our Christian instincts are then stimulated to "give, instead of the amount saved by our two meals of fasting, perhaps much, much more—ten times more when we are in a position to do it" (Kimball, Conference Report, April 1974, 184.) What a different world this would be if churches, civic organizations, and service agencies throughout the earth simply adopted the full law of the fast, including the payment of a generous fast offering. The hungry would be fed, the homeless would be sheltered, many of the traumas and tragedies of this life would be averted, and individuals everywhere would be possessed of a deepened spirituality and a closeness to God.

I will greatly rejoice in the Lord, my soul shall be joyful in my God; for he hath clothed me with the garments of salvation, he hath covered me with the robe of righteousness.

ISAIAH 61:10

We live in a time when evil is increasing all about us. On every side, the father of lies whispers temptation, and the bright lights of the world's enticements beckon. Prophets since time immemorial have warned us to resist iniquity and stay on the Lord's side. The apostle Paul exhorted us to "put on the whole armour of God, that ye may be able to stand against the wiles of the devil" (Ephesians 6:11). We will be able to withstand the evil day if we have "loins girt about with truth, and having on the breastplate of righteousness; and [our] feet shod with the preparation of the gospel of peace; . . . the shield of faith, . . . the helmet of salvation, and the sword of the Spirit" (Ephesians 6:14–17). Mercy and grace cloak us with the garments of salvation. What joy and rejoicing ought we to feel as we turn to the Lord for protection and safety.

NOVEMBER 9

Who is this that cometh . . . with dyed garments . . . ? Wherefore art thou red in thine apparel, and thy garments like him that treadeth in the winefat? I have trodden the winepress alone.

ISAIAH 63:1, 3

Red is symbolic of victory—victory over the devil, death, hell, and endless torment. It is the symbol of salvation, of being placed beyond the power of all one's enemies. Christ's red apparel symbolizes both aspects of his ministry—his mercy and his justice. Because he has trodden the winepress alone (D&C 76:107; 88:106), he has descended below all things and mercifully taken upon him our stains. In addition, he comes in "dyed garments" as the God of justice, even he who has trampled the wicked beneath his feet. "And the Lord shall be red in his apparel, and his garments like him that treadeth in the wine-vat. . . . And his voice shall be heard: I . . . have brought judgment upon all people . . . and I did tread upon them in mine anger, and their blood have I sprinkled upon my garments, and stained all my raiment; for this was the day of vengeance which was in my heart" (D&C 133:48–51).

NOVEMBER 10

In all their affliction he was afflicted, and the angel of his presence saved them: in his love and in his pity he redeemed them; and he bare them, and carried them all the days of old.

ISAIAH 63:9

So many aspects of the infinite and eternal atoning sacrifice of our Lord and Savior are beyond our mortal grasp. How can one man suffer for the sins of another? How can one man be afflicted by the afflictions of another? How can God take the burdens and weight of our sins and place them upon a perfect, sinless Being? How can someone come back from the dead? How can that person's rise from the tomb affect my ability one day to do the same? These are matters we cannot comprehend, but they are matters that we humbly accept and for which we are immeasurably grateful. Perhaps one day the Almighty will perfect our minds and hearts so that we can begin to understand the marvelous workings of God in our lives. In the meantime, we rejoice in the scriptures, in the words of his prophetic spokesmen, and in the quiet but powerful witness of the Spirit that testifies to our souls that these things are true.

NOVEMBER 11

For since the beginning of the world men have not heard, nor perceived by the ear, neither hath the eye seen, O God, beside thee, what he hath prepared for him that waiteth for him.

ISAIAH 64:4

To wait on the Lord is to exercise hope in him. Waiting on the Lord focuses not on frail and faltering mortals but on a sovereign and all-loving God. Hope is more than worldly wishing. It is expectation, anticipation, assurance. We wait on the Lord, not by sitting and wringing our hands and glancing at our clocks periodically, but rather by exercising patience in his providential hand, knowing that the Father of Lights will soon transform a darkened world in preparation for the personal ministry of the Light of the World (1 Corinthians 1:4–8). To wait on the Lord is to exercise a lively hope that the God who is in his heaven is also working upon and through his people on earth. As it was anciently, so it is in our day: The spiritual regeneration required of individuals and whole societies that results in the establishment of Zion takes place "in process of time" (Moses 7:21).

NOVEMBER 12

But we are all as an unclean thing,
and all our righteousnesses are as filthy rags.
ISAIAH 64:6

The prophets remind us—and we need such reminders frequently—just how lost and frail and weak and unprofitable we are without God and his tender mercies. "And since man had fallen he could not merit anything of himself; but the sufferings and death of Christ atone for their sins, through faith and repentance" (Alma 22:14). We are in truth saved by merit, but not by our own merit. As the scriptures make clear, we are saved only through "the merits, and mercy, and grace of the Holy Messiah" (2 Nephi 2:8; 31:19; Moroni 6:4). We strive to keep the commandments and be loyal disciples of our Lord, but in the end, "it is by grace that we are saved, after all we can do" (2 Nephi 25:23). That is, notwithstanding all we can do, despite all we can do, above and beyond all we can do, our trust and our reliance are rooted in the righteousness of our Redeemer (2 Nephi 2:3).

NOVEMBER 13

But now, O Lord, thou art our father; we are the clay, and thou our potter; and we all are the work of thy hand.

ISAIAH 64:8

God is our Father, the divine Potter in whose hands we are clay. He is shaping us into the sons and daughters he would have us become. The Potter forms the clay of our individual lives, and then we are given opportunities to be refined in the kiln of life's experiences and vicissitudes. We can learn and become softened and wiser, or we can become bitter and angry. This life is a school, a place to be taught the everlasting things and cleansed by the power of the Atonement from the impurities of the world. The Potter's work and glory is to bring about our immortality and eternal life (Moses 1:39)—to have us live the quality of life that he himself enjoys. To that end, if we are humble and prayerful, if we are steadfast and immovable, if we are striving for righteousness each day, in process of time we will inherit all that the Father hath (D&C 132:19–22).

NOVEMBER 14

In those days [the Millennium] there shall be no more thence an infant of days, nor an old man that hath not filled his days; for the child shall not die, but shall live to be an hundred years old.

JST Isaiah 65:20

During the Millennium, the thousand-year reign of the King of kings on earth, there will be no death as we know it. There will be no infant mortality, no anguish over a loved one diminishing in capacity incident to aging, no grieving for a dear companion who has been taken unexpectedly. Rather, during those glorious years, the earth will be renewed and receive its paradisiacal, terrestrial glory, and life on earth will be of a different order entirely. When the Savior comes in glory, mortals will continue to live as mortals until they reach the age of one hundred, at which time they will be "changed in the twinkling of an eye" (D&C 43:32; 63:51; 101:28–31). That is, they will pass through death and be transformed from mortality to resurrected immortality instantaneously. Knowing these things and the glory that awaits us, we are constrained to exclaim with John the Revelator, "Even so, come, Lord Jesus" (Revelation 22:20).

The wolf and the lamb shall feed together, and the lion shall eat straw like the bullock. . . . They shall not hurt nor destroy in all my holy mountain, saith the Lord.

ISAIAH 65:25

Who among us can fathom what it will be like to dwell on an earth without fear and strife, hunger and crime, class distinctions and mayhem? Who can picture a world in which all persons are converted to the Lord, in which there are no disputations among people, in which we have all things in common, in which the inhabitants of this sphere are all "made free, and partakers of the heavenly gift"? (4 Nephi 1:3). These are the divine descriptors of the Millennium. In the words of the Savior himself, "All things shall become new, that my knowledge and glory may dwell upon all the earth. And in that day the enmity of man, and the enmity of beasts, yea, the enmity of all flesh, shall cease from before my face. And in that day whatsoever any man shall ask, it shall be given unto him. And in that day Satan shall not have power to tempt any man" (D&C 101:25–28).

NOVEMBER 16

Before I formed thee in the belly I knew thee; and before thou camest forth out of the womb I sanctified thee, and I ordained thee a prophet unto the nations.

JEREMIAH 1:5

Much has been given us by a loving Heavenly Father, and therefore he expects much of us. We are here to fulfill our divine destiny and to bless others with love and the light of the gospel. President James E. Faust said, "It has been said that this church does not necessarily attract great people but more often makes ordinary people great. . . . Any man or woman who enjoys the Master's touch is like potter's clay in his hands. More important than acquiring fame or fortune is being what God wants us to be. Before we came to this earth, we may have been fashioned to do some small good in this life that no one else can do. . . . If God has a work for those with many talents, I believe he also has an important work for those of us who have few" (*Ensign,* May 1994, 5–6).

NOVEMBER 17

Then said I, Ah, Lord God! behold, I cannot speak: for I am a child. But the Lord said unto me, Say not, I am a child: for thou shalt go to all that I shall send thee, and whatsoever I command thee thou shalt speak.

JEREMIAH 1:6–7

Jeremiah's response to his prophetic call is the same question that Moses (Exodus 3:11) and Enoch (Moses 6:31) asked God at the time of their call. "Who am I," Jeremiah seems to be asking, "to do such a mighty thing? Who am I to speak on behalf of the Almighty? Why have I been chosen when there are surely more spiritual and seasoned men in Jerusalem?" God seems little concerned with Jeremiah's perceived inabilities because He knows something of Jeremiah's capabilities; He knows what Jeremiah can do when blessed and empowered. The Lord's response to Jeremiah is much like His response to Enoch, counsel that applies equally to each of us: "Go forth and do as I have commanded thee, and no man shall pierce thee. Open thy mouth, and it shall be filled, and I will give thee utterance. . . . Behold my Spirit is upon you, wherefore all thy words will I justify" (Moses 6:32–34).

NOVEMBER 18

My people have committed two evils; they have forsaken me the fountain of living waters, and hewed them out cisterns, broken cisterns, that can hold no water.

JEREMIAH 2:13

One of the tragic ironies of our day is that so many are dying of thirst while the saving waters of life are within reach. Some are not aware that deliverance is available. Others, sad to say, are not even aware that they thirst. Most of earth's inhabitants have forsaken the Lord. All people thirst, even if they are unaware of their needs. Most people pursue their quest for the living water inappropriately—choosing alternate paths, often employing irresponsible, unproductive, and empty strategies. The world may have its agenda; the Savior has another approach entirely. There is safety and security only in doing things the Lord's way. Our souls are satisfied only as we imbibe the divine draught offered by the dispenser of living water.

NOVEMBER 19

Turn, O backsliding children, saith the Lord; for I am married unto you: and I will take you one of a city, and two of a family, and I will bring you to Zion: and I will give you pastors according to mine heart, which shall feed you with knowledge and understanding.

JEREMIAH 3:14–15

The Bridegroom calls out to his bride, to his people, to his chosen ones. He calls upon them to be gathered home safely into the fold, yoked with him, and linked by covenant with the Saints of the Most High. Jehovah reminds us that conversion is an individual matter, that a nation may be born in a day, but that nation will come into the Church and kingdom one baptism at a time, one endowment and sealing at a time. It is the collection of those possessed of an individual witness of the work that leads to the formation of a mighty people. Those who come into the fold gain new friends, receive callings and assignments as part of their investment in the faith, and are nurtured in the good word of God by caring and inspired Church leaders and friends (Moroni 6:4). The fruit is thus brought forth, and the good fruit remains (John 15:16).

NOVEMBER 20

Were they ashamed when they had committed abomination? nay, they were not at all ashamed, neither could they blush.

JEREMIAH 6:15

As we study the signs of the times, we soon learn that a society is on a steady decline to destruction when it manifests certain attitudes and behaviors. Wars and rumors of wars indicate that power, not patience, prevails. Men's hearts being hardened or growing cold indicate that natural affections and innate concern for others are fading away. Calling good evil and evil good indicates that a massive confusion of values and a denial of absolute truths are well underway. And, finally, when a people become both shameful and shameless in their speech and actions, we know that the Light of Christ within them is being quenched. Their inability to blush is but a sign, a signal that they no longer hold sacred time-honored values and no longer feel embarrassed by their shameless expressions. They have ripened in iniquity and are ready to be swept off the land, according to the scriptural pattern and promises.

NOVEMBER 21

The harvest is past, the summer is ended, and we are not saved.

JEREMIAH 8:20

So very often individuals live today as if there were no tomorrow. They go about their duties with precious little concern for their immortal soul or the consequences of their actions. But we have been placed on earth to "improve our time" (Alma 34:33). We will pass this way only once. Samuel the Lamanite scolded the Nephites of his day with these searing words: "Your days of probation are past; ye have procrastinated the day of your salvation until it is everlastingly too late, and your destruction is made sure; yea, for ye have sought all the days of your lives for that which ye could not obtain; and ye have sought for happiness in doing iniquity, which thing is contrary to the nature of that righteousness which is in our great and Eternal Head" (Helaman 13:38). Indeed, this life is the season appointed for us to prepare to meet God (Alma 34:32).

O Lord, I know that the way of man is not in himself: it is not in man that walketh to direct his steps.

JEREMIAH 10:23

Wise men and women readily acknowledge that they are not smart enough to run their own lives. We treasure the counsel of parents, leaders, and friends, to be sure, but even with that combined wisdom we fall short. The first step in solving our problems, as the apostle Paul said, is "not to think of [ourselves] more highly than [we] ought to think" (Romans 12:3). The second step is to learn to turn to the one Being who knows all things, the One who has known us longest and now knows us best. We know, deep down, that the best course is to allow the Captain of our soul to have sway, so that He can make us into new creatures far beyond anything we might achieve in our own unaided way. "Men and women who turn their lives over to God will discover that He can make a lot more out of their lives than they can" (*Teachings of Ezra Taft Benson,* 361).

Therefore, behold, the days come . . . that it shall no more be said, The Lord liveth, that brought up the children of Israel out of the land of Egypt; but, The Lord liveth, that brought up the children of Israel from . . . all the lands whither he had driven them.

JEREMIAH 16:14–15

Jehovah's deliverance of the children of Israel out of their Egyptian bondage has stood for millennia as the grand illustration of what can happen when the Lord intervenes in behalf of his covenant people. It was and is the greatest of all gatherings, at least for now. For a time is coming, and it will be largely millennial, when the gathering of people throughout the earth into the Church of Jesus Christ will be of such a magnitude that it will cause all former gatherings to pale in significance. That is why the risen Lord spoke to his American Hebrews of the day when the work of the Father [the work of gathering] will "commence" (3 Nephi 21:26, 28; 2 Nephi 30:7–15). Millions upon millions will yet hear the glad tidings, be touched by the power of the Holy Spirit, congregate with the faithful, and complete the process of gathering through receiving the covenants and ordinances of the house of the Lord.

NOVEMBER 24

I the Lord search the heart, I try the reins, even to give every man according to his ways, and according to the fruit of his doings.

JEREMIAH 17:10

We are now in the second act of a three-act play. We are in our second estate to be tutored and tested, to prove ourselves worthy of celestial inheritance. The Lord provides opportunities for us to learn and grow while in mortality. And because we cannot recall our premortal estate (where we were also learning and growing) and we have yet to experience the postmortal world, this is all we have, all we can know right now, all we can do something about. This life is the time for us to be "anxiously engaged in a good cause, and do many things of [our] own free will, and bring to pass much righteousness; for the power is in [us], wherein [we] are agents unto [our]selves. And inasmuch as [we] do good [we] shall in nowise lose [our] reward" (D&C 58:27–28). The Lord knows our heart, our desires and efforts, and he will extend to each of us his perfect mercy and justice.

NOVEMBER 25

Behold, as the clay is in the potter's hand, so are ye in mine hand, O house of Israel.

JEREMIAH 18:6

We are as potter's clay in the hands of the Lord. This simple and vivid metaphor teaches us that we are to be pliable in the Lord's hands as he shapes us into the people he would have us become. He wants us to become as he is, to develop the attributes of godliness, to be found worthy to inherit all that he has. It also means that we must remain pliable in his hands as he bends and shapes us through the growing experiences of life. Implicit in the metaphor is the truth that pottery, once dried and fired, cannot be reshaped—it is now solid and immovable. Like fired clay, we are to be unswerving in our commitment to the Lord, valiant and true to the truth, resolute and unbending in keeping our gospel covenants. True disciples of Christ encompass dual virtues: flexible and firm, submissive and strong, soft and steadfast, unassuming and unwavering. Let us be as clay in the Lord's hands.

For who hath stood in the counsel of the Lord[?] . . . I have not sent these prophets, yet they ran. . . . But if they had stood in my counsel, and had caused my people to hear my words, then they should have turned them from their evil way.

JEREMIAH 23:18–22

Jeremiah lived at a time when false prophets roamed the land uttering empty and incorrect oracles. The word translated here as *counsel* is rendered as *council* in alternate translations. This changes the meaning of the passage appreciably. The manner of determining the validity of a professing prophet becomes "Who among you has stood in the council of God, as I have? Who among you has received his mission and commission directly from the Lord, as I have? If you had received your assignment and authority from the Almighty, as I have, you would be calling people to repentance, not giving them a false sense of security." As Paul wrote, "The spirits of the prophets are subject to the prophets" (1 Corinthians 14:32).

NOVEMBER 27

And ye shall seek me, and find me,
when ye shall search for me with all your heart.
JEREMIAH 29:13

The passage of scripture that inspired young Joseph to offer his first vocal prayer echoes down the decades with power and clarity: "If any of you lack wisdom, let him ask of God, that giveth to all men liberally, and upbraideth not; and it shall be given him" (James 1:5; see Joseph Smith–History 1:11–14). As he said to ancient Israel, the Lord says to us, "Draw near unto me and I will draw near unto you; seek me diligently and ye shall find me" (D&C 88:63). As we diligently come unto the Lord, we will find comfort and peace; we will find answers to prayers and the patience to wait upon the Lord; we will find that faith, hope, and charity become more and more a part of our lives. The promise is sure: We will find the Lord as we come unto him with full purpose of heart.

NOVEMBER 28

Yea, I have loved thee with an everlasting love: therefore with lovingkindness have I drawn thee.

JEREMIAH 31:3

The love of our Heavenly Father and Savior is perfect, constant, and never failing. We learn about their love through Christ. Elder Jeffery R. Holland said, "Jesus did not come to improve God's view of man nearly so much as He came to improve man's view of God and to plead with them to love their Heavenly Father as He has always and will always love them. The plan of God, the power of God, the holiness of God, yes, even the anger and the judgment of God they had occasion to understand. But the love of God, the profound depth of His devotion to His children, they still did not fully know—until Christ came" (*Ensign,* November 2003, 72). We know that "God so loved the world, that he gave his only begotten Son, that whosoever believeth in him should not perish, but have everlasting life" (John 3:16). God's everlasting love for his children gives the faithful the promise of everlasting life.

NOVEMBER 29

I will put my law in their inward parts, and write it in their hearts; and will be their God, and they shall be my people.

JEREMIAH 31:33

The Lord, through Jeremiah his prophet, promised to make a new gospel covenant with Israel. It would bring them into the Lord's presence so that—with changed hearts—all might truly know him. Paul used this prophecy of Jeremiah to show that Christ promised to make a new covenant with Israel (Hebrews 8:10), but the covenant found no enduring acceptance in Jesus' day. Today it is offered anew in the dispensation of the fulness of times. Today the covenant of salvation—the fulness of the gospel—is embraced by increasing numbers of believers as the message of the new and everlasting gospel covenant spreads across the earth. Those who come to the Lord, meekly accept his gospel truth, and wholeheartedly covenant to keep his commandments are promised salvation in his kingdom. And the glorious and full effect of the Lord's covenant promised through Jeremiah will take place during the coming millennial day.

NOVEMBER 30

Behold, I am the Lord, the God of all flesh: is there any thing too hard for me?

JEREMIAH 32:27

Nothing is impossible for God, and "with God nothing shall be impossible" for us (Luke 1:37). He is the omnipotent Father, the great Master of the universe, the God of heaven and earth. To him we owe our lives and everything that we have, including the very air we breathe. "Behold, are not the things that God hath wrought marvelous in our eyes? Yea, and who can comprehend the marvelous works of God" (Mormon 9:16). God's most marvelous work and wonder is us, his spirit sons and daughters. We can fulfill the measure of our creation because we are endowed with something of divinity within us. We can do more than we think we can, we can repent and overcome the world, we can forgive and move forward with faith—all because he is our Father. He wants us to develop the attributes of godliness and attain the fulness of his glory. Nothing is too hard for our Heavenly Father.

December

Surely the Lord God will do nothing, but he revealeth his secret unto his servants the prophets.

Amos 3:7

DECEMBER 1

The Lord hath brought forth our righteousness: come, and let us declare in Zion the work of the Lord our God.

JEREMIAH 51:10

The happiest people are those who are engaged in activities that stretch their minds, bodies, or spirits to their limits in an effort to accomplish something worthwhile, something meaningful. That's why missionaries are often so happy. They've never worked harder, but they've never been happier. The paradox of happiness is that it's not reserved for the chosen, lucky few—happiness is available to all who unselfishly lose themselves in the service of others. Opportunities to bless others and build Zion are all around us. Happiness will come as we forget about ourselves and roll up our sleeves and get to work—with a burning desire to put our trust in the Lord, help others, and share the gospel. When we "put [our] shoulder to the wheel" (*Hymns,* no. 252) in worthwhile endeavors, we do the work of the Lord and discover the path to greater happiness.

DECEMBER 2

The Lord is good unto them that wait for him, to the soul that seeketh him.
LAMENTATIONS 3:25

Meditation is a lost art in our hectic, hurry-up world. Our days are full of busyness and earnestness, with to-do lists that seem to grow longer each day. The words of Alma are provident: "Let all thy doings be unto the Lord, and whithersoever thou goest let it be in the Lord; yea, let all thy thoughts be directed unto the Lord; yea, let the affections of thy heart be placed upon the Lord forever" (Alma 37:36). Take time to wait silently before God. Read scriptures, and let them speak to you. Pray, and listen. Let the Spirit whisper to your heart that you are God's greatest creation, that you are loved, that you matter. Feel his divine love and compassion. God will give you a fresh start, a new beginning, another chance, if you stop complaining, stop fighting, stop resisting. Surrender to him and accept his love and grace. Sit silently, and seek diligently. Pour out your soul and then quietly wait.

DECEMBER 3

I will give them one heart, and I will put a new spirit within you; and I will take the stony heart out of their flesh, and will give them an heart of flesh: . . . they shall be my people, and I will be their God.

EZEKIEL 11:19–20

Along with the prophecies of the scattering and exile of Israel, the Lord, through his prophets, continually renewed his promise of a latter-day gathering, assuring the faithful that his plans would not be thwarted and in time would all be fulfilled. At that glorious day, the faithful will be of "one heart," and a "new spirit" will be given them. An unreceptive "stony heart" will be replaced by a receptive "heart of flesh" (Ezekiel 11:19). We live in that day of gathering. We gather as we exercise faith, repent, and become truly converted. We gather as we become "new creatures" in Christ and become alive in Christ (Mosiah 27:26; 2 Nephi 25:25). We gather as we heed the promptings of the Holy Ghost and shun evil. We gather as we serve and worship together, without falsehood or deception, as Saints of the living God—since true conversion always results in true worship of the Lord. Our authentic gathering to Zion is manifest in a soft and receptive heart.

Take thee one stick, and write upon it, For Judah . . . then take another stick, and write upon it, For Joseph, the stick of Ephraim . . . and join them one to another into one stick; and they shall become one in thine hand.

EZEKIEL 37:16–17

The magnificent chapter 37 of Ezekiel bears testimony of three realities that are in many ways one and the same. First of all, Ezekiel bears testimony of the actuality of the physical resurrection, the time in which each one of us will rise from the grave, our spirit and body becoming inseparably connected. Another truth is also taught through this emphasis on the resurrection: Ezekiel also bears witness that God will gather together the tribes of Israel. Just as the Fall is typified by the scattering of Israel, even so the Atonement and Resurrection are typified by the gathering of Israel. The eventual union of Judah and Ephraim is typified by the coming together (or "growing together"; 2 Nephi 3:12) of the Bible, or stick of Judah, and the Book of Mormon, or stick of Ephraim. Truly, as the apostle Paul testified, all things are gathered together in one in Christ (Ephesians 1:10).

DECEMBER 5

And they shall teach my people the difference between the holy and profane, and cause them to discern between the unclean and the clean.

EZEKIEL 44:23

Prophets and other righteous leaders and fellow-citizens in the household of faith can teach us much about the power of discernment. We can know what is from God and what is from Satan by looking at the source, the motivation, and the result—whether or not they lead us "to do justly, and to love mercy, and to walk humbly with thy God" (Micah 6:8). That which is of God inspires us to do good (Alma 5:40–41). Spiritual discernment develops as we learn to shun evil and seek righteousness by feasting upon the scriptural words of eternal life; it grows in us as we follow worthy examples of those who take time for holiness and turn away from sin; it comes as we humbly live worthy of the Spirit so that the light of spiritual discernment will guide us in this world of gathering darkness. We will not be deceived as we follow the Lord and his anointed apostles and prophets and hearken to the voice of the Spirit.

DECEMBER 6

But Daniel purposed in his heart that he would not defile himself with the portion of the king's meat, nor with the wine which he drank.

DANIEL 1:8

Daniel's life was one of firm commitment. He had made up his mind about the Lord and his commandments long before he was taken captive into Babylon. Firm commitment means being disciplined one day at a time, over the long haul. Firm commitment requires being alert to subtle temptations and enticing allurements that would get us off the gospel path. Firm commitment means we have integrity of heart whether alone or in public. Daniel was rock solid in his commitment to the Lord even as he faced King Nebuchadnezzar. He knew that kings and monarchs come and go, but the Lord and his truth is everlasting. And he knew that the days of mortality are fleeting—who we are in our heart of hearts determines our peace and joy here and hereafter. Because of Daniel's faithfulness and integrity, God gave him knowledge, understanding, and wisdom beyond all others. Let us be people of firm commitment.

DECEMBER 7

But there is a God in heaven that revealeth secrets.

DANIEL 2:28

King Nebuchadnezzar was troubled because of a vivid dream that left him unable to sleep. No one could interpret the dream but Daniel—a humble man with a spiritual gift. If it is the Lord's will, and if the seeker is righteous in his desires, the Lord will send light and knowledge. Sister Mary Ellen Smoot, then general president of the Relief Society, observed: "God can and does reveal secrets to the faithful. How precious an opportunity is this. How wonderful that it actually happens. I testify that our prayers, offered in humility and sincerity, are heard and answered. It is a miraculous thing, but it is real" (*Ensign,* November 2000, 89). Indeed, the power of prayer is awesome and authentic.

DECEMBER 8

If it be so, our God whom we serve is able to deliver us from the burning fiery furnace. . . . But if not, be it known unto thee, O king, that we will not serve thy gods.

DANIEL 3:17–18

There is no doubt that most stories in scripture (and many in everyday life) that entail the exercise of faith in pressure-packed situations have happy endings. Almost always when people show their faith in the Lord and demonstrate their discipleship, the Lord manifests his kindness and delivers them from the current crisis. But our faith needs to be deep enough and sound enough that we follow the Lord even in the face of the worst of circumstances and the severest of consequences. Like Job, we must be willing to trust God, even if the Almighty should choose to slay us (Job 13:15). Our faith in the Lord Jesus Christ and the hope of eternal life that flows from it must be of such a magnitude that no matter the cost, we will be true. Indeed, the law of sacrifice calls upon us to offer our all to God and his kingdom, even our own lives if necessary.

I saw in the night visions . . . one like the Son of man came with the clouds of heaven, and came to the Ancient of days. . . . And there was given him dominion, and glory, and a kingdom, . . . an everlasting dominion, which shall not pass away.

DANIEL 7:13–14

Daniel 7:13–14 is a passing reference to the great council to be held at Adam-ondi-Ahman just before the coming of the Son of Man in glory. In this council, all who have held the keys of the kingdom will give an accounting, each in his turn back to Adam, who will then account to the Lord Jesus Christ: "The Son of Man stands before [Adam], and there is given him [Christ] glory and dominion. Adam delivers up his stewardship to Christ, that which was delivered to him as holding the keys of the universe but retains his standing as head of the human family" (Smith, *Teachings,* 157; see also D&C 116). In addition, on this occasion a monumental sacrament meeting will take place, one in which such scriptural luminaries as Moroni, Elias, John the Baptist, Elijah, Abraham, Isaac, Jacob, Peter, James, John, and "all those whom [the] Father hath given [Christ] out of the world" (D&C 27:14) will be in attendance.

And the Lord said to Hosea, Go, take unto thee a wife of whoredoms and children of whoredoms: for the land hath committed great whoredom, departing from the Lord. So he went and took Gomer the daughter of Diblaim.

HOSEA 1:2–3

The Old Testament story of Hosea contains an odd mixture of tragedy and hope. It appears that Hosea was commanded to marry an immoral woman. Despite her profligate behavior, however, Hosea remained true and faithful to his marriage covenant. Read as a literal account, this story is a grand tribute to the prophet Hosea. It is also a touching metaphor for the Bridegroom's steadfast love and patience for his wandering bride. Literal or metaphorical or both, this story provides a message of hope similar to that of the allegory of Zenos: God simply will not let Israel go! "God does not look on sin with allowance," the Prophet Joseph Smith affirmed, "but when men have sinned, there must be allowance made for them" (*Teachings,* 240–41). Indeed, "There is never a time when the spirit is too old to approach God. All are within the reach of pardoning mercy, who have not committed the unpardonable sin" (*Teachings,* 191).

DECEMBER 11

Sow to yourselves in righteousness, reap in mercy; break up your fallow ground: for it is time to seek the Lord, till he come and rain righteousness upon you.

HOSEA 10:12

What we sow with effort and perseverance and humility here in this mortal probation, we will reap in the eternities to come. "One must be impressed with the great message of the Lord's law of the harvest," said Elder L. Tom Perry. "His system produces growth, multiplication, and abundant rewards. Surely as we watch the blessings of this growth cycle each year, we would expect His children to catch the vision of their mortal potential" (*Ensign,* November 2000, 89). In the process of becoming all that our Heavenly Father would have us become, we experience growing pains, and we make mistakes; we learn and grow and have opportunities to become more committed and consecrated to discipleship. Indeed, true spirituality is manifest in kindness and mercy, in devotion to truth, in living a life of integrity. This life is the time to sow in charity and righteousness so that we can reap the harvest of everlasting life.

DECEMBER 12

Turn unto the Lord your God; for he is gracious and merciful, slow to anger, and of great kindness, and he will turn away the evil from you.

JST Joel 2:13

Turning to the Lord changes us. We become new creatures, different people. Sincere followers of the Lord have no disposition for evil, no desire to hurt or harm, no hypocrisy and hidden agendas. That does not mean they are perfect, without sin and shortcomings, foibles and faults. These true disciples are also mortal; they live in a fallen world; they constantly strive to put off the natural man and become Saints (Mosiah 3:19). Although they "have sinned, and come short of the glory of God" (Romans 3:23), their hearts are attuned to the Spirit; their every desire is to bless others, overcome the temptations of the world, and endure to the end. As we humbly turn to the Lord, he will strengthen us in our trials and fortify our resolve to turn away from evil. Christ can change our hearts, our lives.

DECEMBER 13

I will pour out my spirit upon all flesh; and your sons and your daughters shall prophesy, your old men shall dream dreams, your young men shall see visions.

JOEL 2:28

As Joseph Smith was praying to God in September 1823, an angelic messenger surrounded by light appeared in his room. The angel spoke of a book written upon plates of gold that was deposited in a hill in the state of New York; those plates, when translated, became the Book of Mormon, Another Testament of Jesus Christ. The angel quoted to Joseph various verses and prophecies from the Bible, among which was Joel 2:28–32 (Joseph Smith–History 1:41). The prophet Joel prophesied of the time in which we live, a time when the Lord would pour out his Spirit upon all flesh, a time when prophecy would increase in the land and Zion would prosper. Since the restoration of the gospel, the Spirit of the Lord has inspired people in the world to accomplish things almost unbelievable to those who behold them—all in preparation for the Savior's return.

DECEMBER 14

The Lord dwelleth in Zion.

JOEL 3:21

Zion is a holy community, a fortification of the Saints, and a refuge against the evils of our day. It is any place where the people of the covenant throughout the earth gather to the stakes of Zion for safety and shelter (D&C 101:17–21). "It shall come to pass that the righteous shall be gathered out from among all nations, and shall come to Zion, singing with songs of everlasting joy" (D&C 45:71). Zion is a state of being, a state of righteousness for "THE PURE IN HEART" (D&C 97:21). The Lord surely dwells in the hearts of his faithful disciples, but he also dwells in the midst of his earthly kingdom. This is his Church, and we are his people if we are obedient, humble, and steadfast in keeping our covenants and enduring in faithfulness. We do our part to build Zion when we strive to live the gospel and share it with others.

Surely the Lord God will do nothing, but
he revealeth his secret unto his servants the prophets.
AMOS 3:7

In every dispensation, the Lord works through prophets when he has a work to perform and truth to reveal. Now, as in times past, we need the steady and reassuring voice of the Lord's anointed prophet who will show us the way to spiritual safety. The prophet is the only man on earth who possesses and exercises all the keys of the priesthood (D&C 132:7). He is the mouthpiece of God for the Church; what he says is what the Lord would say (D&C 1:38; 68:4). We have the promise that the Lord will never allow his prophet to lead the people astray. Great blessings come from faithfully following him. What a comfort it is to know that the Lord speaks to us today through a living prophet. What a blessing to know that we have a clear voice we can trust to declare the mind and will of the Lord. Truly, we thank God for a prophet to guide us in these latter-days (*Hymns,* no. 19).

DECEMBER 16

Woe to them that are at ease in Zion.

AMOS 6:1

The devil wants to lead us down the pathway of apathy and slothfulness. He knows that if we settle into a state of indifference and laziness, we are his. Nephi said, "And others he will pacify, and lull them away into carnal security, that they will say: All is well in Zion; yea, Zion prospereth, all is well—and thus the devil cheateth their souls, and leadeth them away carefully down to hell. . . . Therefore, wo be unto him that is at ease in Zion!" (2 Nephi 28:21–24). We are to be on guard against evil in all its forms and ever aware of temptation and the wiles of the adversary. But we must also beware of the pride of apathy, of the smugness of idleness. The devil doesn't have to tempt us with wickedness or ensnare us in overt sin. It is enough if we are lulled into apathy.

DECEMBER 17

*Behold, the days come, saith the Lord God,
that I will send a famine in the land, not a famine of bread, nor
a thirst for water, but of hearing the words of the Lord.*
AMOS 8:11

The downfall of Israel and the early Christian church was foretold anciently by Amos the prophet. The darkness of apostasy would eventually cover the land, as pride, wickedness, and indifference crowded out light and truth. We have a similar famine today as people search for truth and cannot find it; they seek for peace and it eludes them; they yearn for joy and it escapes them. But an abundance of truth, peace, and joy is to be discovered all around us. Truth is found as we heed the words of the Lord that come by listening to the living oracles and reading the scriptures. Peace is found as we turn our hearts to God in sincere prayer and live worthy of the influence of the Spirit. Joy is found in service to our brothers and sisters in the family of God across the earth. There is no famine to the righteous.

DECEMBER 18

And saviours shall come up on mount Zion.
OBADIAH 1:21

President Gordon B. Hinckley spoke of how we can overcome selfishness and become saviors on Mount Zion: "The element of selfishness crowds in upon us constantly. We need to overcome it, and there is no better way than to go to the house of the Lord and there serve in a vicarious relationship in behalf of those who are beyond the veil of death. . . . We have no assurance that they will accept that which we offer. But we go, and in that process we attain to a state that comes of no other effort. We literally become saviors on Mount Zion. . . . Just as our Redeemer gave His life as a vicarious sacrifice for all men, and in so doing became our Savior, even so we, in a small measure, when we engage in proxy work in the temple, become as saviors to those on the other side who have no means of advancing unless something is done in their behalf by those on earth" (*Ensign,* November 2004, 105).

DECEMBER 19

Arise, go to Nineveh, that great city,
and cry against it; for their wickedness is come up before me.
JONAH 1:2

Jonah was sent to preach the gospel of repentance to the people of Nineveh. He himself needed to repent of his recalcitrance and become more submissive to the will of the Lord. We likewise are called upon to be courageous as we proclaim the good news of the gospel to the world—a world in desperate need of the Lord and his saving truths. Elder Russell M. Ballard said: "Lucifer is unleashing vulgar, revolting, violent, and sleazy filth with the design to destroy the spiritual sensitivity of our Father's children. We truly are at war with those who mock God and shun the truth, so let us keep our covenants and heed our call to service. Let us marshal all of the Lord's resources, including the power of our own testimonies. Let them be heard by many more people" (*Ensign,* November 2000, 77). It may not always be easy or convenient, but when the Lord and his servants call—we must respond, willingly, humbly, and with courage.

And God saw their works, that they [the people of Nineveh] turned from their evil way and repented; and God turned away the evil that he had said he would bring upon them. But it displeased Jonah exceedingly, and he was very angry.

JST JONAH 3:10–4:1

Jonah was a prophet of God, but he was also a human. He knew something about the people of Nineveh—their reputation for cruelty and their evil style of living—and he wanted nothing to do with them. After God had dramatically gotten his attention, Jonah reluctantly preached repentance to Nineveh, and his worst nightmare came to pass: The people actually repented! Jonah became angry to the point of pouting at God. This story teaches us to have our hearts purified to the extent that we rejoice in good things that come to others. In this case, an extremely wicked nation was turned from their waywardness by the power of the word. Like the sons of Mosiah, when our hearts are right, we do not want anyone to perish, much less to suffer the pains of hell (Mosiah 28:3). When we are possessed of the love of God, we rejoice in the recovery of any of God's lost sheep (1 Corinthians 13; Moroni 7).

What doth the Lord require of thee, but to do justly, and to love mercy, and to walk humbly with thy God?
MICAH 6:8

The Lord's standard of righteousness remains unchanged in every generation: Do good works and treat people fairly, extend mercy and forgiveness to others, and be meek and humble. "The Lord requireth the heart and a willing mind; and the willing and obedient shall eat the good of the land of Zion in these last days" (D&C 64:34). If we want a place in Zion with the fellowship of the Saints and in celestial glory with those who have their names written in heaven (D&C 76:68), we must live with integrity, be compassionate and kindhearted, and submissively seek to do the will of the Lord. That is the gospel in action. The everlasting gospel is not found in pontificating and theorizing, nor in debating and speculating. The essence of what the Lord requires of us is simply *living* the gospel with full purpose of heart—a soft and sympathetic heart, a meek and merciful heart, a gracious and generous heart.

DECEMBER 22

The Lord is slow to anger, and great in power . . . : [he] hath his way in the whirlwind and in the storm, and the clouds are the dust of his feet.

NAHUM 1:3

Life is filled with heartache and difficulty. We face the whirlwinds of disease, disaster, and death; we experience storms of irritations and ill-treatment. Two things should comfort us in the midst of these tempests. First, we all experience them. Second, we all need them. The massive blows and shattering blasts (not to mention the small, invariable frustrations of life) can humble us and turn our hearts to God and everlasting things. They can also have the opposite effect—turning our hearts to anger and bitterness. Just as the Lord's presence can be seen and felt in the natural world around us, he certainly can be present in our individual lives, in the heartrending contingences of daily living. As we turn to the Lord with full purpose of heart, we will find comfort, rest, and peace to our souls.

DECEMBER 23

For the earth shall be filled with the knowledge of the glory of the Lord, as the waters cover the sea.

HABAKKUK 2:14

The knowledge of God shall continue to cover the earth as the gospel of Jesus Christ is preached to the world's inhabitants now and in the coming millennial day. All Israel will gather to the ensign of nations and find peace, strength, and salvation in the kingdom of God. Temples are beginning to dot the earth and will increase during the Millennium, when there will be even more holy places in which priesthood ordinances essential to salvation and eternal life can be performed in uninterrupted calm. We are encouraged to seek deeply and broadly to gain knowledge of both heavenly and earthly things (D&C 88:77–79). As we grow in our testimony of eternal truth and then share it with others, we do our part to fill the earth with the knowledge of God.

DECEMBER 24

The Lord thy God in the midst of thee is mighty; he will save, he will rejoice over thee with joy; he will rest in his love, he will joy over thee with singing.
ZEPHANIAH 3:17

The ruler of the synagogue went to Jesus, pleading for help for his dying daughter. While he spoke to the Master, those of the ruler's household arrived and said: "Thy daughter is dead: why troublest thou the Master any further? As soon as Jesus heard the word that was spoken, he saith unto the ruler of the synagogue, Be not afraid, only believe" (Mark 5:35–36). That is the message of salvation: Have faith and go forward with confidence in the Lord and his miraculous, redeeming power. We live in a world where fear and anxiety abound, but in this troubling day, we must remember to "look to God and live" (Alma 37:47). We cannot let Satan, the father of fear, divert us from faith in the Lord and from faithful living. When we are fearful, we hold back, we fail to commit fully, we let doubt and hesitation take the place of faith. Satan's method is fear and doubt; the Lord's is faith and hope.

DECEMBER 25

Thus saith the Lord of hosts; Consider your ways.

HAGGAI 1:7

The prophet Haggai's admonition to the people of his day to consider their ways relative to the rebuilding of the temple also applies to our day. Do we give of our time and resources to build the kingdom? Do we regularly attend the temple and pay our tithes and offerings so that temples can be built in greater numbers across the earth? Do we manifest the pure love of Christ in our thoughts and deeds? We need to look into our hearts, examine ourselves whether we be in the faith, as Paul counseled (2 Corinthians 13:5), to see how we stand with the Lord and the things of everlasting worth. The Lord will not bless us if we do not heed his commands (D&C 82:10; 130:20–21). Now is the time to consider your ways, to ponder deeply the purposes of life and God's plan for you, to take action on the things you may need to change. Consider your ways.

Rejoice greatly, O daughter of Zion.
ZECHARIAH 9:9

President Gordon B. Hinckley said: "Put on thy beautiful garments, O daughters of Zion. Live up to the great and magnificent inheritance which the Lord God, your Father in Heaven, has provided you. Rise above the dust of the world. Know that you are daughters of God, children with a divine birthright. Walk in the sun with your heads high. Know that you are loved and honored, that you are part of His kingdom, and that there is for you a great work to be done which cannot be left to others" (*Ensign,* November 1983, 84). It is gospel light that gives us comfort and direction, peace and contentment in this life. An abiding testimony of the Father's great plan of happiness for us, his children, empowers us to climb the mountains of mortality with courage and steadfastness. Yes, we'll have our sorrows and setbacks, and we'll have our joys and triumphs. Surely the Lord will strengthen us as we rise to the divinity within us.

DECEMBER 27

As for thee also, by the blood of thy covenant I have sent forth thy prisoners out of the pit wherein is no water.
ZECHARIAH 9:11

The covenant of the Father, made to all of his spirit children before the foundations of the world, was that he would send a Savior to redeem us from our sins and deliver us from death. It is the plan of the Father that every individual have the opportunity to hear the fulness of the gospel, either in this life or in the life to come. The preaching of the gospel goes forward hereafter, just as it does here. In that postmortal spirit world, however, there is no provision made for baptism by water; that sacred ordinance, which has everlasting implications, must be performed on earth. We therefore perform a labor of love in holy temples in baptismal fonts on this side of the veil in behalf of those who dwell in a world who do not have access to that regenerational ordinance.

DECEMBER 28

But who may abide the day of his coming? and who shall stand when he appeareth? for he is like a refiner's fire, and like fullers' soap.

MALACHI 3:2

At some future date, the Messiah will return to the earth in power and glory. Satan will be bound and have no influence over the hearts of those who remain on earth (1 Nephi 22:26). The coming of Christ will usher in the millennial era of peace, joy, and righteousness. The righteous Saints will be "quickened" and will join those "who have slept in their graves," who will also "be caught up to meet him in the midst of the pillar of heaven" (D&C 88:96–97). The glory of the Lord's "consuming fire" (Hebrews 12:29) will destroy the wicked and sanctify the righteous. The cleansing power of his presence will purify the earth. It will be a great day for the righteous and a terrible day for the wicked. We prepare for this coming day by obeying the commandments, living with charity and integrity, standing in holy places, and seeking the Spirit for our guide (D&C 45:57).

DECEMBER 29

Will a man rob God? Yet ye have robbed me. But ye say, Wherein have we robbed thee? In tithes and offerings.

MALACHI 3:8

The Lord has given us life and the very air we breathe; he has blessed us with this beautiful earth filled with his wonders; he has bestowed upon us his great plan of happiness by which we can have peace here and eternal life hereafter. Our hearts overflow with thankfulness for the bounties of life. We show our gratitude to God for his goodness by willingly paying our tithes and offerings so that the work of the kingdom of God can move forward. We manifest our reverent appreciation by being honest and generous in our offerings. We rob God, the giver of all gifts, when we close our hearts to opening our wallets. The Lord is not concerned about amounts and totals; but he is very concerned about our hearts. The kingdom will continue to roll forth without any of our contributions, but we need the consecration and humility that come from offering of our means.

DECEMBER 30

The day cometh, that shall burn as an oven; and all the proud, yea, and all that do wickedly, shall be stubble: . . . that it shall leave them neither root nor branch.

MALACHI 4:1

At the second coming of the Lord, the proud and the wicked will be destroyed as the earth is purified. Every corruptible and impure thing that belongs to Babylon will be cleansed from the earth at the Lord's return in glory (D&C 64:24; 101:24–25). Those who reject the Savior because of the pride of their hearts, as well as the slothful who are not valiant in their testimony of Jesus, will be cut off from their ancestry and posterity, severed from their family tree. There is safety, peace, and everlasting joy with their families for those who gather to Zion and diligently follow the Lord.

DECEMBER 31

Behold, I will send you Elijah the prophet before the coming of the great and dreadful day of the Lord: and he shall turn the heart of the fathers to the children, and the heart of the children to their fathers, lest I come and smite the earth with a curse.

MALACHI 4:5–6

Moroni explained to the Prophet Joseph that Elijah the prophet would be sent to "plant in the hearts of the children the promises made to the fathers, and the hearts of the children shall turn to their fathers" (D&C 2:2). Because Elijah came to the Kirtland Temple in April 1836 (D&C 110), there comes into the hearts of the Saints a desire to enjoy the promises made to Abraham, Isaac, and Jacob—the gospel, the priesthood, and eternal life (Abraham 2:8–11). In addition, through the spirit of Elijah we sense the need and desire to make those same blessings available to our more immediate fathers, those who died without a knowledge of the fulness of the gospel. These blessings come only through the ordinances of the temple. Through the ministry of Elijah and the sacred labor of the Saints of God in holy temples, an eternal link is established between ancestry and posterity, thus enabling the earth to fulfill its foreordained purpose.

Sources

"The Family: A Proclamation," *Ensign,* November 1995, 102.

Ballard, M. Russell. *Ensign,* November 2000, 75, 77.

Benson, Ezra Taft. Conference Report, April 1988, 3.

———. *Teachings of Ezra Taft Benson.* Salt Lake City: Bookcraft, 1988.

Cowley and Whitney on Doctrine. Comp. Forace Green. Salt Lake City: Bookcraft, 1963.

Evans, Richard L. Evans. *Richard L. Evans Quote Book.* Salt Lake City: Deseret Book, 1971.

Eyring, Henry B. *Ensign,* November 2000, 86; *Ensign,* May 2004, 17.

Faust, James E. *Ensign,* May 1994, 5–6; *Ensign,* November 2000, 59; *Ensign,* May 2004, 51.

Hinckley, Gordon B. *Ensign,* November 1983, 84; *Ensign,* August 1988, 4; *Ensign,* November 1993, 60; *Ensign,* November 1994, 53; *Ensign,* November 2000, 52; *Ensign,* November 2003, 113–14; *Ensign,* May 2004, 112, 115; *Ensign,* September 2004, 4; *Ensign,* November 2004, 4, 105.

———. *New Era,* January 2002, 6–7.

———. *Teachings of Gordon B. Hinckley.* Salt Lake City: Deseret Book, 1997.

Holland, Jeffrey R. *Ensign,* November 2000, 39; *Ensign,* May 2002, 64; *Ensign,* November 2003, 72.

———. *New Era,* October 1980, 15

Hunter, Howard W. *That We Might Have Joy.* Salt Lake City: Deseret Book, 1994.

Hymns of The Church of Jesus Christ of Latter-day Saints. Salt Lake City: The Church of Jesus Christ of Latter-day Saints, 1985.

Journal of Discourses. 26 vols. London: Latter-day Saints' Book Depot, 1854–86.

Kimball, Spencer W. *Circles of Exaltation.* Devotional address, Brigham Young University, Provo, Utah, 28 June 1968.

———. Conference Report, April 1974, 184.

———. *Ensign,* March 1976, 72.

Maxwell, Neal A. *Ensign,* November 2000, 36–37.

McConkie, Bruce R. *Choose an Eternal Companion.* Devotional address, Brigham Young University, Provo, Utah, 3 May 1966.

———. Conference Report, October 1973, 57.

Monson, Thomas S. *Ensign,* November 2000, 66; *Ensign,* May 2004, 23, 55–56.

Nelson, Russell M. *Ensign,* November 1989, 22.

Oaks, Dallin H. *Ensign,* November 2000, 32.

Old Testament Student Manual. 2d ed. 2 vols. Salt Lake City: The Church of Jesus Christ of Latter-day Saints, 1981–82.

Packer, Boyd K. Conference Report, October 1986, 20.
———. *Ensign,* May 1992, 67.
Perry, L. Tom. *Ensign,* November 2000, 89.
Rasmussen, Ellis T. *A Latter-day Saint Commentary on the Old Testament.* Salt Lake City: Deseret Book, 1993.
Scott, Richard G. *Ensign,* November 2000, 27.
Smith, Joseph. *Teachings of the Prophet Joseph Smith.* Selected by Joseph Fielding Smith. Salt Lake City: Deseret Book, 1976.
Smoot, Mary Ellen W. *Ensign,* November 2000, 89.

About the Authors

Lloyd D. Newell and Robert L. Millet are members of the Religious Education faculty at Brigham Young University and coauthors of *Jesus, the Very Thought of Thee, When Ye Shall Receive These Things,* and *Draw Near Unto Me.*

Brother Newell teaches classes at BYU in the department of Church History and Doctrine and in the School of Family Life. He has served as the announcer and writer for the Mormon Tabernacle Choir broadcast "Music and the Spoken Word" since 1990 and is the author of several books, including *The Divine Connection* and *May Peace Be with You.* He and his wife, Karmel H. Newell, are the parents of four children.

Brother Millet, professor of ancient scripture and former dean of Religious Education at BYU, has served with Church Public Affairs and the Materials Evaluation Committee of The Church of Jesus Christ of Latter-day Saints. He is the author of numerous books, including *Grace Works, Are We There Yet?* and *When a Child Wanders.* He and his wife, Shauna Sizemore Millet, are the parents of six children.